International Markets for Enterprise Software Vendors

Jay Greenwald

International Revenue *ACCELERATION*
www.intl-rev-acceleration.com

DISCLAIMER: THE AUTHOR PUBLISHER HAS USED BEST EFFORTS IN PREPARING THIS BOOK. THE AUTHOR PUBLISHER DOES NOT MAKE ANY REPRESENTATION OR WARRANTY AS TO THE ACCURACY OR COMPLETENESS OF THE CONTENTS OF THIS BOOK AND DISCLAIMS ANY IMPLIED WARRANTIES OF MERCHANTABILITY OR FITNESS FOR A PARTICULAR PURPOSE. THE INFORMATION HEREIN IS NOT WARRANTED TO PRODUCE ANY PARTICULAR RESULTS AND THE ADVICE AND STRATEGIES MAY NOT BE SUITABLE FOR EVERY READER. THE AUTHOR PUBLISHER SHALL NOT BE LIABLE FOR ANY LOSS OF PROFIT OR ANY OTHER DAMAGES INCLUDING SPECIAL, INCIDENTAL OR CONSEQUENTIAL DAMAGES.

NOTE: THIS BOOK IS INTENDED TO PRESENT GENERAL INFORMATION ON INTERNATIONAL MARKETS FOR ENTERPRISE SOFTWARE VENDORS. ALTHOUGH THE INFORMATION PRESENTED IS VIEWED TO BE RELIABLE AND UP TO DATE, SOME MATERIAL MAY BE IMPACTED BY LOCAL CUSTOMS OR CHANGES IN PROFESSIONAL OR INTERNATIONAL STANDARDS SINCE THE MANUSCRIPT WAS COMPLETED. IF SPECIFIC ADVICE IS NEEDED, READERS ARE ENCOURAGED TO OBTAIN SERVICES FROM A PROFESSIONAL IN THIS FIELD.

ISBN: 1463534620
ISBN-13: 978-1463534622

DEDICATION

To my wife Wendy, who has always been tolerant of my travel
all over the world, 41 countries so far.
Also to my 3 daughters Jenny, Jess and Julia who are always encouraging and
supportive.

CONTENTS

1   Executive Overview   1

2   Introduction   5

3   Europe   23

4   East Asia   47

5   Latin America   89

6   Canada, Australia,   113
    New Zealand

7   The Rest of the   123
    World

8   Summary – Entire   131
    World

9   About the Author   133

   Notes   135

1 EXECUTIVE OVERVIEW

This book explores how enterprise software vendors generally consider expansion of their sales and channels outside their home countries, with a bias toward U.S.-based software companies. It introduces a framework for country evaluation using the following 4 Dimensions to analyze and rank countries for desirability:

1. Wealth as measured by gross domestic product (GDP) at purchasing power parity (PPP)
2. Acceptance of technology
3. Acceptance of English as a language of commerce
4. The technology sales and buying culture

A U.S. enterprise software vendor typically launches its international expansion into Europe, then East Asia, then Latin America. However, many are starting their expansion into East Asia sooner, sometimes even before Europe, because the East Asian economies are growing and developing rapidly. East Asian growth didn't even pause as the U.S. and Europe suffered through the financial crisis of 2008–2009.

Despite its rapid development and growing importance to the world economy, East Asia is a more challenging locale for U.S. and European enterprise software vendors because of the diversity of its countries: economies, population, cultures, rivalries, vast geographical area, and business practices foreign to Westerners. However, technology and software vendors cannot afford to delay their expansion into these growing and challenging markets.

This book divides the world into five major regions and the Rest of the World for analysis.

Region	How Important	% of World GDP[i]	% of World Population	% of World Software Sales[ii]
United States (U.S.)	Crucial	19.8%	4.5%	40.0%
Europe	Crucial	20.5%	7.3%	37.3%
East Asia	Important → Crucial, rapid development, influence growing	33.3%	51.1%	13.2%
Latin America	Low → Medium importance, uneven but strong development, influence growing	8.5%	7.9%	1.8%
Canada, Australia, New Zealand	Medium importance, rich like U.S. and Europe, but small	3.1%	0.9%	4.4%
Other: <ul><li>Russia</li><li>Eastern Europe</li><li>Asia from Turkey to Pakistan</li><li>Middle East</li><li>Africa</li></ul>	Low importance	14.8%	28.3%	3.4%

Figure 1 – Five Major Regions of the World

The conclusion this book reaches—based on extensive international enterprise software sales, channel, go-to-market, and merger and acquisition (M&A) experience—is that most enterprise software companies from the U.S. expand within the major regions in the following order:

1. **Europe** – The UK and the rest of Northern Europe first. The "Rest of Northern Europe" is: (1) Scandinavia + Finland (2) Belgium, Netherlands and Luxembourg, hereafter referred to as "Benelux." After Northern Europe most enterprise software vendors expand into France and Germany, then Spain and Italy. The smaller countries and Eastern Europe are last.

2. **East Asia** – There are more variations to the order of market entry for this region of the world, but in many cases the order is: (1) Singapore and its Southeast Asian orbit of rapidly developing Malaysia and Indonesia first (2) followed by Korea and Japan (3) last is Greater China (Mainland, Hong Kong, Taiwan), and India.

3. **Latin America** – Brazil, followed by Mexico and Argentina with Chile, and the remaining smaller countries last.

4. **Canada, Australia, New Zealand** – Canada first as an extension of the U.S., even before Europe. Australia and New Zealand as a unit at approximately the same time as Singapore and Southeast Asia.

Organization of This Book

Chapter 2, Introduction, defines "enterprise software," explains the 4 Dimensions of Country Evaluation for enterprise software vendors to assess countries for market entry, introduces country analysis, and then divides the world into regions for analysis.

Then, there is a section for each region of the world, which evaluates countries on the 4 Dimensions and the typical order an enterprise software vendor enters each of the markets and regions:

Chapter 3, Europe – page 23

Chapter 4, East Asia – page 47

Chapter 5, Latin America – page 89

Chapter 6, Canada, Australia, and New Zealand – page 113

Chapter 7, The Rest of the World – page 123.

2 INTRODUCTION

Once an enterprise software vendor starts to consider selling and marketing its products outside its home country, where should it begin? Or if the software vendor has already started sales in some regions of the world, which countries or regions should it expand into next?

This book discusses the sales environment and suitability by country or region of the world for on-premise enterprise, Software as a Service (SaaS), and Cloud software vendors to expand and launch their international sales without taking specific products into account. For a custom market entry, channel, go-to-market, and/or start-up implementation plan for international launch tailored specifically to a software vendor's products and stage of international sales evolution, contact International Revenue *ACCELERATION* (www.intl-rev-acceleration.com).

This book then outlines a proven methodology for analyzing countries and market entry order for a typical enterprise software vendor expanding its sales into new countries. It introduces a general framework for enterprise software vendors to analyze and understand regions of the world based on country analysis. Then, it uses this framework to analyze the markets of Europe, East Asia, Latin America, and the other countries of the world.

Definition of Business and Enterprise Software Used in This Book

Although consumers and small businesses are using and adopting technology at an accelerating rate, enterprise software is a sophisticated product. When this book refers interchangeably to *business* or *enterprise* software, it refers to software for larger companies, which is more advanced than the basic products that make a PC work (operating systems, web browsers, Microsoft Office applications, simple databases) and basic micro-business software (accounting, customer relationship management). Some examples of enterprise software are:

- **Data Center Software**
  Managing a business's IT computing environment, such as backup, storage management, and network/server management. Some examples of vendors that sell this type of software are VMware, EMC Corporation, Hewlett Packard's server and network management products, and many products from CA Technologies. Also in this category are Microsoft's server operating systems and collaboration products, as well as IBM's mainframe operating systems, and system software products.

- **Enterprise Application Development Tools**
  Database software from Oracle or Informix, IBM's application/web server products, and many tools from ASG Software Solutions and BMC Software. There are also SaaS tools emerging in this segment such as Rally Software Development's agile software.

- **Software to Optimize Functional Areas of Enterprise Organizations**
  Customer Relationship Management (CRM) for managing sales or customer support. Another example is accounting software for general ledger or cash management. A subset of this is software to optimize business processes, supply chains/logistics, and project management— most of which is industry-specific.

- **Software to Manage Entire Business Operations**
  Enterprise Resources Planning Software (ERP) and Enterprise Business Applications, like Oracle and SAP, across many industries. There are numerous smaller software vendors who offer industry-specific versions of ERP products.

The target markets and prospects for these kinds of business software products are medium and large enterprises, both businesses and other large organizations, including governments and non-profits. The starting point for businesses and other organizations large enough to buy enterprise software varies by country. However, the minimum hardware configuration for an entity to consider enterprise software is one server. It is more likely that a good target organization would have multiple servers and more than twenty desktops.

4 Dimensions for Country Evaluation

To be a strong market for enterprise software, a country needs a minimum level of wealth and technology acceptance, which are the most important dimensions for country evaluation. Level of economic development is also important; if many people in a country are concerned about basic sustenance, the country will not be a strong market for enterprise software. As for technology acceptance, if high-speed Internet access from a computer is not within reach for most people and businesses, that country is probably not a good market for targeting enterprise software sales.

A good indicator for evaluating a country's enterprise software market is to track its evolution over three stages of technology adoption:

1. **Basic** – PC infrastructure exists: PC operating systems, peer-to-peer networking, and basic productivity software;

2. **Mid-Level** – PC networking with basic servers. Enterprise-level software such as enterprise resource planning (ERP) and customer relationship management (CRM) software becomes established. High-speed Internet is widely available in the major cities and businesses centers;

3. **Advanced** – many medium and most enterprise businesses have data centers. Workers access business systems with smartphones and tablets. High-value software solutions such as server virtualization, collaboration software, business intelligence, and analytics are prevalent.

For most types of enterprise software, countries in stages two and three in the list immediately above (hereafter referred to as *Mid-Level* and *Advanced* stages of technology adoption) are the first choices for enterprise software vendors to initiate their international sales expansion.

The other two dimensions for consideration are: (1) acceptance of the English language, and (2) the technology sales and buying culture, which are described in more detail below.

To be more precise, the following 4 Dimensions are evaluated in this book for enterprise software vendors when considering where to expand their sales efforts:

1. Wealth

Gross Domestic Product (GDP) per person in a country is a measure of wealth and is also an excellent indicator for acceptance of technology. Purchasing Power Parity (PPP) is the measure of GDP used in this book, which is a country's GDP adjusted for the local price of a common basket of goods. The lower the prices, the higher the GDP is adjusted because each unit of economic output is worth the same compared to other countries with higher prices. Adjusting for PPP removes the effect of short-term currency fluctuations and is the one of the best economic indicators to use for measuring the demand for enterprise software products for medium-sized and large enterprises around the world. If the GDP PPPs for two countries are equivalent, a larger population with high Internet usage indicates a more desirable market for enterprise software.

2. Acceptance of Technology

This is related to the stage of technology adoption a country has attained: *Basic*, *Mid-Level* or *Advanced*. Certainly, if high-speed Internet access is not widespread for business use, or if a high percentage of people are living in poverty, then the target market for enterprise software (medium and enterprise businesses) will not be substantial enough.

Technology acceptance is related to wealth, but there are some areas of the world where acceptance and use of technology has raced ahead. Some examples:

- **Internet usage and access**
  Internet usage approaches 90% of the population in the Scandinavian region, with Finland being one of the highest in the world. Also, high Internet speeds enable businesses to exploit IT technology and encourage customers to use Internet and mobile apps. South Korea has an average download connection speed of almost forty mpbs (megabits per second), driven by centralized government planning and a high percentage of the population residing in urban areas. By comparison, the average Internet access speed of the U.S. is ten mbps, ranked thirty-second in the world.[iii]

- **Mobile phone usage**

  Some countries, such as Singapore and Israel, have 150 cell phones for every 100 people, as many people have both a personal and a business mobile phone. In Asian countries such as Japan and China, Internet access is more often from mobile phones than from PCs, because users do not have the space for a PC (Japan) or access to a PC (China). In much of East Asia, mobile Internet access has exceeded PC access for several years—even before the widespread adoption of smartphones.

The two indicators above are signs of an advanced technology market where enterprise software will be in demand on a broad scale.

Quantitatively, two measures will be used to qualify Acceptance of Technology:

1. **Total Software Market Size** – from the World Information Technology and Services Alliance's (WITSA) *Digital Planet 2010* report;

2. **The Network Readiness Index** (NRI) – this is from the World Economic Forum's *Global Information Technology Report*. Also used will be a custom index built from a subset of the NRI indicators to measure "readiness to embrace enterprise software." See footnote number [xii] on page 135 and **Figure 8** on page 22.

To be a viable candidate for international expansion, a necessary condition is that a country/region passes the screening for both the *Wealth* and *Acceptance* of *Technology* dimensions for country evaluation.

3. Acceptance of English as a Language of Commerce

English is the dominant language in the technology industry and the most widely spoken language in the business world. As an indicator of the widespread usage of English, the number of Wikipedia articles in English is 3.5 million—more than three times any other language. To operate in the U.S., Canada, UK, Australia, India, New Zealand, Ireland, Singapore, South Africa, and the Philippines, software vendors must provide their software in English.

An approach employed by many U.S. software vendors considering their international expansion is to test the English-speaking markets first. As a result, the expense of software translation can be incurred over time and it will be easier to determine the order of language translation.

4. The Technology Sales and Buying Culture

This dimension is less exact and quantifiable than the other three, but it is still worth considering qualitatively. The index for measurement is the similarity of the target market's technology evaluation and buying practices to the U.S., Canada (hereafter called North America[iv]), and the large European countries. These are the leading technology markets in the world. This dimension also measures the all-important supply of local sales and technical people for staffing an international sales operation.

Using North America and Europe as a benchmark for measurement does not imply superiority. These areas are simply dominant in enterprise software sales, so it follows that they would be the most attractive for enterprise software vendors to consider for expansion.

Country Analysis for Enterprise Software

This section divides the world into its major regions and compares the relative economic output of the regions and their wealth as measured by GDP PPP per person. Statistics used to measure technology acceptance are also illustrated throughout, such as software market sizes and Internet usage.

The best approach to evaluate territorial expansion for enterprise software is to divide the world into the U.S. plus four major regions. Then subdivide the remaining territory into (1) Canada, Australia and New Zealand (2) The Rest of the World, which is the sixth item in the list below:

1. **United States (U.S.)**

2. **Europe**

3. **Latin America**

4. **East Asia**

5. **Canada, Australia, New Zealand**

6. **The Rest of World**, which is: Russia, Eastern Europe, Asia (from Turkey to Pakistan), Middle East, Africa, and the Caribbean region.

   Russia is the largest country in this group and represents the "R" in the informal alliance of countries called BRICS.[v] The five BRICS countries (Brazil, Russia, India, China and recently added South

Africa) are rapidly growing and developing countries. Combined, the BRICS countries contain 42% of the world's population. These countries have formed the BRICS alliance to collectively increase their diplomatic and economic influence and power. However, none of these countries are usually early destinations for enterprise software vendors to consider expansion, as is explained throughout this book.

Other than Russia, in this group of countries, there are a few small, noncontiguous territories with rapid growth on their way to becoming advanced technologically, such as Israel, South Africa, and possibly a few others in the Arab Middle East. The remaining countries in this group are considered developing countries. No negative connotation is intended; however, these developing countries are usually the last expansion targets for enterprise software vendors.

Economic and Population Comparisons

Examining the world by the regions outlined above, **Figure 2** shows 2010 GDP PPP, population, and GDP PPP per person[vi], which is an indicator for wealth.

	GDP - PPP		Nominal GDP		Population (millions)		GDP / Person
	US$ (billion)	% of World	US$ (billion)	% of World	(million)	% of World	US $
World	$ 74,004	100.0%	$ 61,963	100.0%	6,901	100.0%	$ 10,724
Euro. Union	$ 15,151	20.5%	$ 16,106	26.0%	501	7.3%	$ 30,242
U.S.	$ 14,624	19.8%	$ 14,624	23.6%	312	4.5%	$ 46,857
East Asia	$ 24,644	33.3%	$ 16,139	26.0%	3,530	51.1%	$ 5,952
Latin America	$ 6,259	8.5%	$ 4,644	7.5%	546	7.9%	$ 11,463
Canada, Australia, N.Z.	$ 2,332	3.2%	$ 2,922	4.7%	60	0.9%	$ 38,738
Rest of World	$ 10,994	14.9%	$ 7,528	12.1%	1,952	28.3%	$ 5,632

Figure 2 – REGIONS OF THE WORLD: 2010 GDP and Population

Figure 3 reflects the same information graphically:

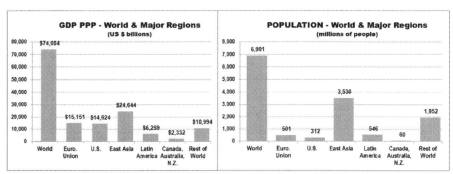

Figure 3 – REGIONS OF THE WORLD: 2010 GDP PPP and Population Comparison

These graphs clearly show the high total GDPs of Europe and the U.S. compared to their comparatively small populations, which is indicative of high GDPs per person. They also show how much East Asian GDP has grown, magnified by the adjustment for PPP. China accounts for 41% of total East Asia GDP. Its economy is now 70% of the size of the U.S., measured by GDP PPP. China continues to expand at an annual rate of 9% per year, as it has for the last 30 years. Some economists believe China is overheating, and that its rate of growth is unsustainable. The prediction is that China's economy will be constrained by asset bubbles, inflation, shortages of raw materials, environmental damage, and increased pressure on its infrastructure.

In terms of extremes in country size and wealth, East Asia exhibits far more variation than either Europe or Latin America. Here are some illustrations of these East Asian contrasts and extremes:

- It includes a tiny country and a special administrative region of China with some of the highest GDPs per person in the world (Singapore, Hong Kong).

- East Asia has several countries with GDPs per person of approximately US $30,000 (Japan, Taiwan, South Korea).

- China, with its huge population, has GDP PPP per person of US $7,500, approximately 75% of the world's average GDP per person.

- India is poor but rapidly growing with a GDP per person of US $3,300. Its population is forecasted to pass China's in the next twenty years to become the most populous nation in the world.

The East Asian countries encompass a much larger geography than European or Latin American countries, and many have had rivalries for centuries. Their cultures span thousands of years and they have vanquished and occupied each other time and time again. In many cases mutual distrust has escalated into hatred. However, this doesn't stop them from doing business with each other.

Within the four major regions, the countries that make up Europe and Latin America are culturally similar, whereas the East Asian countries are much more diverse. The cultural similarity of European and Latin American countries within their own regions translates into homogeneous enterprise software buying patterns. In contrast, East Asian buying patterns and decision making are unlike anywhere else in the world, with contrasts between each country that are opaque to non-natives. This can be difficult for sales managers from the West to comprehend, because sometimes there is no real answer to the question of when an enterprise software deal will close.

Examining GDP per person on a country level, the U.S., Europe, Canada, and Australia/New Zealand stand out as the wealthiest regions. Throughout this book, the per capita GDP of countries will be represented using the categories described in **Figure 4**:

Category	GDP PPP per Person Range (US $)	Examples with World Rank and 2010 GDP PPP per Person (US $)
Poor → **Developing** (102 countries, according to IMF[vii])	<$1,000 – $9,999	**Congo** – 182nd in the world, $340 GDP per person **Zimbabwe** – 181st at $395 ↓ **Colombia** – 83rd at $9,445
Middle Income (37 countries)	$10,000 – $19,999	**S. Africa** – Ranked 76th, $10,505 GDP per person **Brazil** – 71st at $11,289 ↓ **Poland** – 44th at $18,837

Category	GDP PPP per Person Range (US $)	Examples with World Rank and 2010 GDP PPP per Person (US $)		
Upper Middle Income *(19 countries)*	$20,000 – $29,999	**Portugal** – Ranked 40th, $23,113 GDP per person **Saudi Arabia** – 39th at $23,742 ↓ **South Korea** – 25th at $29,971 **Spain** – 26th at $29,651 **Israel** – 28th at $29,404		
Wealthy *(16 countries)*	$30,000 – $39,999	**Japan** – Ranked 24th, $33,828 GDP per person **France** – 23rd at $34,092 ↓ **Sweden** – 14th at $37,775 **Australia** – 9th at $39,962		
Top Countries[viii]	Above $40,000	1. **Qatar** 2. **Luxembourg** 3. **Singapore** 4. **Norway** 5. **Brunei** 6. **U.S.** 7. **Hong Kong**[ix] 8. **Switzerland** 9. **Netherlands**	$ 88,232 GDP per person $ 80,304 $ 57,238 $ 52,238 $ 47,200 $ 47,123 $ 45,277 $ 41,765 $ 40,777	

Figure 4 – GDP PPP Per Person Categories for Countries

Technology Acceptance

The wealthiest countries have the highest level of technology acceptance and are the countries at the *Advanced* stage of technology adoption. **Figure 5** illustrates the key indicators for technology acceptance: software market sizes and Internet usage, along with GDP PPP and population data. It is sorted by total software market size:

| Country | GDP per Person / Total GDP | # People (million) | Total Software Market | | | Internet Users | | |
			2010 Market / Tech Adoption	2010-13 Forecasted Growth		Actual (million)	World Rank	% of People
U.S.	$46,900 $14,630 billion	312	$130.0 bill. advanced	5.4%		240	2	77%
Ger-many	$35,800 $ 2,930 billion	82	$21.6 billion advanced	8.8%		65	6	80%
UK	$35,300 $ 2,180 billion	62	$21.3 billion advanced	9.5%		51	7	83%
China	$7,500 $10,080 billion	1,343	$16.7 billion mid-level	12.3%		420	1	31%
France	$32,600 $ 2,150 billion	66	$15.4 billion advanced	9.5%		45	9	68%
Japan	$33,800 $ 4,310 billion	127	$14.2 billion advanced	4.1%		99	3	78%
Benelux	$39,800 $ 1,110 billion	28	$12.0 billion advanced	11.5%		23	21	84%
Scandi-navia + Finland	$39,400 $ 1,000 billion	25	$11.1 billion advanced	11.7%		22	22	87%
Italy	$29,200 $ 1,770 billion	61	$10.0 billion advanced	9.6%		30	14	50%
Canada	$38,800 $ 1,330 billion	34	$ 9.8 billion advanced	5.8%		26	12	76%

Country	GDP per Person / Total GDP	# People (million)	Total Software Market			Internet Users		
			2010 Market – Tech Adoption	2010-13 Forecasted Growth		Actual (million)	World Rank	% of People
Spain	$29,300 $ 1,350 billion	46	$ 9.1 billion advanced	11.8%		29	15	63%
Austra-lia	$39,000 $ 882 billion	23	$ 4.0 billion advanced	7.0%		17	25	75%
Brazil	$11,400 $ 2,180 billion	191	$ 2.8 billion mid-level	6.4%		72	5	38%
South Korea	$30,000 $ 1,460 billion	49	$ 2.7 billion advanced	7.9%		39	11	81%
Singa-pore	$57,100 $ 290 billion	5	$ 1.1 billion advanced	7.7%		3	58	67%
Hong Kong	$45,300 $ 320 billion	7	$ 0.5 billion advanced	7.6%		5		69%

Figure 5 – Summary of GDP, Population, Total Software Markets[x], Internet Usage[xi]

Of course, software market size in a country is one of the best indicators to assess for expansion. **Figure 6**, below, indicates worldwide share of total software sales by region. *Total software* consists of:

1. **Enterprise Software** – for medium and enterprise-sized businesses, the subject of this book
2. **Small Business Software**
3. **Consumer Software**

The data source for the following charts, the World Technology and Services Alliance, estimates the worldwide total software market at US $325 billion. Gartner Group, a well-known IT market research consultancy, estimates the 2010 worldwide *enterprise software* market at US $245 billion or approximately 75% of worldwide total software. Each country's split between sales of consumer, small business, and enterprise software varies. The less developed countries tend to have lower shares of enterprise software as a percentage of their total software markets. For example, according to Gartner, China's enterprise software accounts for 35% of its total software market, much lower than the worldwide share of enterprise software at 75% of total software. China is between the *Basic* and *Mid-Level* for technology adoption and Gartner characterizes the Chinese software market as "still relatively young and evolving."

Graphically, **Figure 6** illustrates percentages of total software market sizes in 2010 and 2013 for the major regions of the world, adjusting for the size of the market growth forecasted for 2010 – 2013:

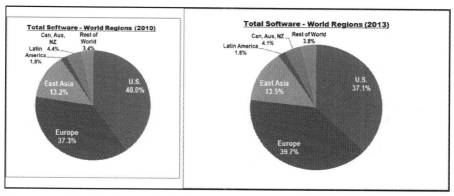

Figure 6 – Total Software Market Sizes by Region of the World, 2010 and 2013

Figure 6 indicates that the U.S. software market is 40% of world's total; the remaining 60% is outside of the U.S. This portion is forecasted to increase to 62.9% of the world's total by 2013. Europe's share of the worldwide software market is forecasted to increase from 37.3% to 39.7% of the world's total by 2013, which will exceed the U.S.'s forecasted share of 37.1% by then. East Asia is forecasted to increase from 13.2% to just 13.3% of the world's software market, despite China alone increasing from 5.1% to 5.8% in 2013.

Looking at Internet usage from the sixth column of **Figure 5**, on page 16, contrast the number of Internet users in the developed countries with the vast numbers of Internet users in the BRICS countries below:

China	420 million Internet users (more than the population of the U.S.!)
India	81 million
Brazil	76 million
Russia	60 million
South Africa	5 million
Total BRICS countries	**642 million**

More of the Internet usage in the advanced countries listed in **Figure 5** above is for advanced tasks such as smartphone access/Apps, E-commerce, SaaS, and accessing corporate applications, whereas a high percentage of the Internet usage in the BRICS countries and the rest of the less developed world is from older cell phones that do not have the capabilities for advanced usage.

Another strong indicator of both technology acceptance and the sales and buying culture for enterprise software is the World Economic Forum's Networked Readiness Index[xii] (NRI), which rates and tracks country information and communications technology (ICT) environments on a scale of 1–7, low to high. According to the World Economic Forum's *Global Information Technology Report* (see footnote [xiii] on page 136), the NRI index is built from the enabling factors for countries to fully benefit from new technologies in IT and communications in their competitive strategies and their citizens' daily lives.[xiii] The index is compiled by ranking 71 indicators (thirty-two from quantitative measurements and thirty-nine from qualitative measures), gathered from the WEC Executive Opinion Survey spanning 138 countries. A real strength of the NRI is its consistent data and methodology across these 138 countries, which increases the validity of comparisons between them.

The following table, **Figure 7,** ranks the NRI scores for the top thirteen countries along with other selected countries, using the NRI indices from 2010–2011. It also lists the NRI index rankings from four years ago. Those countries that moved up or declined more than eight places are in bold in the fifth column, "Change in Rank." The table also shows the country rankings for the three major sub-indices that are made up of the 71 indicators that form the NRI. The definitions of the sub-indices are in the footnotes at the end of this book, starting on page 135.

Country	NRI Index	NRI World Rank		Change in Rank: 2007–11	NRI Sub-Indices – World Rank		
	1–7 (LO–HI)	2010 –2011	2006 –2007		Environ.[xiv]	Readiness[xv]	Usage[xvi]
Sweden	5.60	1	2	↑1	1	3	3
Singapore	5.59	2	3	↑1	4	1	4
Finland	5.43	3	4	↑1	3	2	6
Switzerland	5.33	4	5	↑1	2	5	15
U.S.	5.33	5	7	↑2	14	8	5
Taiwan	5.30	6	13	↑7	19	7	2
Denmark	5.29	7	1	↓6	10	9	7
Canada	5.21	8	11	↑3	5	15	14
Norway	5.21	9	10	↑1	6	20	11
South Korea	5.19	10	19	↑9	27	17	1
Netherlands	5.19	11	6	↓5	7	19	10
Hong Kong	5.19	12	12	---	12	11	13
Germany	5.14	13	16	↑3	16	14	12
UK	5.12	15	9	↓6	9	31	9
Australia	5.06	17	15	↓2	13	26	16
New Zealand	5.03	18	22	↑4	15	23	18
Japan	4.95	19	14	↓5	21	38	8
France	4.92	20	23	↑3	18	29	17
Israel	4.81	22	18	↓4	24	27	19

Country	NRI Index 1-7 (LO-HI)	NRI World Rank 2010–2011	NRI World Rank 2006–2007	Change in Rank: 2007–11	NRI Sub-Indices – World Rank Environ.[xiv]	NRI Sub-Indices – World Rank Readiness[xv]	NRI Sub-Indices – World Rank Usage[xvi]
Belgium	4.80	23	24	↑1	22	22	26
Malaysia	4.74	28	26	↓2	36	10	25
China	4.35	36	59	↑23	57	16	36
Spain	4.33	37	32	↓5	37	70	28
Chile	4.28	39	31	↓8	33	47	40
India	4.03	48	44	↓4	58	33	67
Italy	3.97	51	38	↓13	51	64	49
Indonesia	3.92	53	62	↑9	62	39	80
Brazil	3.90	56	53	↓3	66	59	52
South Africa	3.86	61	47	↓14	38	79	83
Turkey	3.79	71	52	↓19	63	81	62
Mexico	3.69	78	49	↓29	69	100	64
Argentina	3.47	96	63	↓33	100	98	85

Figure 7 – Country Rankings: NRI Index for Information & Communications Technology

As a region, the Scandinavian countries plus Finland (Sweden, Denmark, Norway, and Finland) have the highest NRI indices, all in the top ten in the world, with Sweden and Finland ranked first and third, respectively. This is attributable to these countries having the highest Internet and advanced mobile phone usage in the world and strong government planning to create environments conducive to information technology. Another region with strong results and continued growth is the small and now becoming medium-sized "Asian Tigers" (Singapore, Taiwan, South Korea, and China's special administrative region of Hong Kong). These areas have the highest readiness and usage scores of any region, particularly in:

- Advanced mobile usage
- Fastest Internet connections (led by South Korea, with the highest average connection speed in the world at almost forty megabits per second)
- Governments that plan and create receptive environments for companies to do business

High NRI index rankings show a strong correlation with wealth, with twenty-seven out of the top twenty-eight countries encompassing the top 20% having high incomes and only Malaysia, ranked twenty-eighth in the world, not being a high income country. Another example is the rich continent of Europe: ten of its countries are in the top twenty of the NRI rankings. However, small country size seems to have little correlation with higher NRI ranking, which is counterintuitive. Perhaps larger market size and scale overcome the advantages of small size. An example of the advantage of small size is the ease of building fast Internet connections in a small, high-density geography, such as in Singapore, Hong Kong, or South Korea.

The greatest number of large gainers in the NRI rankings over the last four years comes from East Asia:

- Taiwan: 13th → 6th in the world
- South Korea: 19th → 10th
- China: 59th → 36th (23 places!)
- Indonesia: 62nd → 53rd

Furthermore, Singapore and Hong Kong held their places at second and twelfth. Japan's decline has mirrored its economic and population stagnation, but India declining four places is surprising considering its economic development and rapid growth over this four year period. East Asia's performance in the NRI rankings are outstanding.

In the last four years, the most large decliners in the NRI rankings are from Latin America, with its three largest economies all falling in the rankings:

- Brazil: 53rd to 56th in the world

- Mexico: 49th to 78th (29 places!)
- Argentina: 63rd to 96th (33 places in 4 years!)

Even small but progressive Chile declined eight places, from thirty-first to thirty-ninth in the world. The performances of Mexico and Argentina might be expected, as both have been experiencing governmental and economic crises. However, Brazil's decline is puzzling since it has grown so much over the last four years and its future prospects are so bright.

The **Acceptance of Technology** sections for each of the regions below (see page 28 for Europe, page 55 for East Asia, and page 96 for Latin America) will present country values for a custom "readiness to embrace enterprise software" index. This index is developed from a blend of six of the 71 indicators that form the NRI, which are the most relevant to enterprise software vendors considering expansion into new territories. **Figure 8** identifies these six indicators and their weightings:

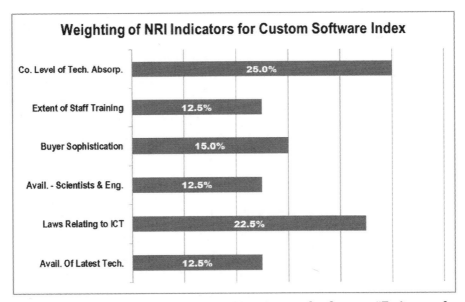

Figure 8 – Weighting of the Selected NRI Indicators for Custom "Embrace of Enterprise Software" Index

3 EUROPE

Introduction

Europe is one the richest areas of the world and one of the most technologically advanced. Politically and economically, twenty-seven of the leading countries have joined together into a loose confederation called the European Union (EU). The EU was intended to unite the economies and monetary policies of its members, however its mission and scope seem to have blurred. A descriptive sentence from Wikipedia highlights the confused mission of the EU: "The EU operates through a hybrid system of supranational independent institutions and intergovernmentally made decisions negotiated by the member states."

The EU laws/regulations and the degree to which EU members are really united is in constant flux. For example:

1. The Common Currency: Euro (€)

    - Seventeen of the twenty-seven members have abolished their old currencies and use the Euro exclusively

    - Seven additional members will start using the Euro once they fulfill entry requirements

    - The UK, Sweden, and Denmark are EU members but have decided to keep their own currencies. Denmark's opt-out might change in the future, whereas the decisions of the UK and Sweden seem more permanent

2. Norway and Switzerland are not EU members but abide by most of the EU business regulations, except those regulations involving

agriculture and fisheries. These countries are considered part of the European Economic Area, not the EU.

From the standpoint of an enterprise software vendor considering entry into European markets, the effect of the EU on business strategies is minor. Some examples:

- **("+")** Pricing products in Euros (except for the UK, Switzerland, and Denmark);

- **("-")** Hiring a non-EU citizen to work in the EU as an employee requires retaining a European lawyer to work through issues proving that the job could not be carried out by an EU citizen;

- **(tiny "-")** Non-EU citizens take longer to get through airports when traveling within Europe. EU citizens must only flash their passports to travel from country to country.

Figure 9 is a map of Europe, showing the status of countries' EU membership:

Figure 9 – Map of Europe with EU Membership Status

Europe: Wealth

Figure 10 shows 2010 GDP PPPs and populations for the top twenty European economies ranked by total GDP PPP[xvii]. The gray stripes are for ease of reading and have no other significance.

GDP Rank		World Rank	GDP using PPP (US $ billions)			World Rank	Population (millions)			GDP (PPP) / Person (calculated)		
			US$ (billion)	% of Europe	% of World		People (millions)	% of Europe	% of World	US $	Europe Rank	Index (Total Euro. = 100)
1.	Germany	5	2,932	18.2%	4.0%	14	81.8	14.6%	1.2%	35,844	9	124
	"U.K. + Ireland"	---	2,355	14.6%	3.2%	---	66.3	11.9%	1.0%	35,520	---	123
2.	U.K.	8	2,181	13.5%	2.9%	22	61.8	11.0%	0.9%	35,291	10	123
3.	France	9	2,146	13.3%	2.9%	21	65.8	11.8%	1.0%	32,614	12	113
4.	Italy	10	1,771	11.0%	2.4%	23	60.6	10.8%	0.9%	29,224	14	101
5.	Spain	13	1,354	8.4%	1.8%	27	46.2	8.3%	0.7%	29,307	13	102
	"Benelux"	---	1,110	6.9%	1.5%	---	27.9	5.0%	0.4%	39,797	---	138
	Scandinavia + Finland	---	997	6.2%	1.3%	---	25.3	4.5%	0.4%	39,407	---	137
6.	Poland	20	718	4.5%	1.0%	34	38.1	6.8%	0.6%	18,845	19	65
7.	Netherlands	21	677	4.2%	0.9%	61	16.6	3.0%	0.2%	40,783	3	142
8.	Belgium	30	393	2.4%	0.5%	76	10.8	1.9%	0.2%	36,389	8	126
9.	Sweden	32	352	2.2%	0.5%	88	9.4	1.7%	0.1%	37,447	6	130
10.	Austria	35	330	2.0%	0.4%	93	8.4	1.5%	0.1%	39,286	4	136
11.	Switzerland	36	325	2.0%	0.4%	94	7.8	1.4%	0.1%	41,667	2	145
12.	Greece	37	323	2.0%	0.4%	74	11.3	2.0%	0.2%	28,584	15	99
13.	Czech Republic	42	261	1.6%	0.4%	78	10.5	1.9%	0.2%	24,857	16	86
14.	Norway	45	256	1.6%	0.3%	116	4.9	0.9%	0.1%	52,245	1	181
15.	Romania	47	252	1.6%	0.3%	54	21.5	3.8%	0.3%	11,721	23	41
16.	Portugal	48	246	1.5%	0.3%	77	10.6	1.9%	0.2%	23,208	17	81
17.	Denmark	49	204	1.3%	0.3%	109	5.6	1.0%	0.1%	36,429	7	126
18.	Hungary	52	188	1.2%	0.3%	84	10.0	1.8%	0.1%	18,800	20	65
19.	Finland	54	185	1.1%	0.2%	112	5.4	1.0%	0.1%	34,259	11	119
20.	Ireland	55	174	1.1%	0.2%	120	4.5	0.8%	0.1%	38,667	5	134
TOTAL - Europe			$ 16,112		21.8%		559		8.1%	$ 28,808		100.0

Figure 10 – Top 20 European Economies Ranked by GDP[XVIII]

Figure 11 below recasts the European countries/regions from highest to lowest GDP per person. It illustrates that most the major European economies have GDP PPP per person in the *Wealthy* range of approximately US $30,000 or greater. These major economies are highlighted with gray bands, as these are usually considered first by enterprise software vendors, having larger economies, larger populations, and a broad target of medium-sized and enterprise organizations for enterprise software:

GDP Rank	GDP using PPP (US $ billions)				Population (millions)				GDP (PPP) / Person (calculated)		
	World Rank	US$ (billion)	% of Europe	% of World	World Rank	People (millions)	% of Europe	% of World	US $	Europe Rank	Index (Total Euro. = 100)
14. Norway	45	256	1.6%	0.3%	116	4.9	0.9%	0.1%	52,245	1	181
11. Switzerland	36	325	2.0%	0.4%	94	7.8	1.4%	0.1%	41,667	2	145
7. Netherlands	21	677	4.2%	0.9%	61	16.6	3.0%	0.2%	40,783	3	142
"Benelux"	---	1,110	6.9%	1.5%	---	27.9	5.0%	0.4%	39,797	---	138
Scandinavia + Finland	---	997	6.2%	1.3%	---	25.3	4.5%	0.4%	39,407	---	137
10. Austria	35	330	2.0%	0.4%	93	8.4	1.5%	0.1%	39,286	4	136
20. Ireland	55	174	1.1%	0.2%	120	4.5	0.8%	0.1%	38,667	5	134
9. Sweden	32	352	2.2%	0.5%	88	9.4	1.7%	0.1%	37,447	6	130
17. Denmark	49	204	1.3%	0.3%	109	5.6	1.0%	0.1%	36,429	7	126
8. Belgium	30	393	2.4%	0.5%	76	10.8	1.9%	0.2%	36,389	8	126
1. Germany	5	2,932	18.2%	4.0%	14	81.8	14.6%	1.2%	35,844	9	124
"U.K. + Ireland"	---	2,355	14.6%	3.2%	---	66.3	11.9%	1.0%	35,520	---	123
2. U.K.	8	2,181	13.5%	2.9%	22	61.8	11.0%	0.9%	35,291	10	123
19. Finland	54	185	1.1%	0.2%	112	5.4	1.0%	0.1%	34,259	11	119
3. France	9	2,146	13.3%	2.9%	21	65.8	11.8%	1.0%	32,614	12	113
5. Spain	13	1,354	8.4%	1.8%	27	46.2	8.3%	0.7%	29,307	13	102
4. Italy	10	1,771	11.0%	2.4%	23	60.6	10.8%	0.9%	29,224	14	101
12. Greece	37	323	2.0%	0.4%	74	11.3	2.0%	0.2%	28,584	15	99
13. Czech Republic	42	261	1.6%	0.4%	78	10.5	1.9%	0.2%	24,857	16	86
16. Portugal	48	246	1.5%	0.3%	77	10.6	1.9%	0.2%	23,208	17	81
6. Poland	20	718	4.5%	1.0%	34	38.1	6.8%	0.6%	18,845	19	65
18. Hungary	52	188	1.2%	0.3%	84	10.0	1.8%	0.1%	18,800	20	65
15. Romania	47	252	1.6%	0.3%	54	21.5	3.8%	0.3%	11,721	23	41
TOTAL - Europe		$ 16,112		21.8%		559		8.1%	$ 28,808		100.0

Figure 11 – Europe GDP per Person, Highest to Lowest

Figure 10 and **Figure 11** introduce the artificial creation of three groups of adjacent and culturally similar countries to consider as units:

1. **UK + Ireland**

   Note that Ireland is a separate sovereign state from the UK, but that Northern Ireland is part of the UK, which consists of England, Wales, Scotland, and Northern Ireland. Geographically, Ireland and Northern Ireland share an island very close to the rest of the UK. The UK and Ireland are similar, but might resist being identified as a unit (similar to the U.S. and Canada). Historically, Ireland had been a separate state from the UK because its population was predominately Catholic, while the other states within the UK were predominantly Protestant. In the modern world, however, this distinction has faded into irrelevancy.

2. **Scandinavia + Finland**

   Norway, Denmark, Sweden (considered Scandinavia) and Finland.

3. **Benelux**

   Belgium, Netherlands, and Luxembourg.

Sometimes the three regions above are collectively called Northern Europe.

Discarding countries that are too small, the artificial units of Benelux and Scandinavia + Finland are at the high range of the *Wealthy* GDP per person category with values near US $40,000 per person, comparable to the wealth of the U.S. at nearly $47,000 per person. These two regions each account for 6% – 7% of total European GDP, which is slightly less than Spain at 8%, the smallest of the five large European economies.

The five largest European economies (Germany, France, UK, Italy, Spain) make up 65% of total European GDP and have GDPs per person in the middle *Wealthy* range, clustered from US $30,000–$36,000. Of these five, Germany and Spain are the outliers in population, with approximately eighty million and forty-five million respectively, while the others are approximately sixty million each. Adding the five large European economies and the regions of Benelux and Scandinavia + Finland implies a software vendor could capture almost 80% of Europe GDP by operating across these seven countries/regions.

Europe: Acceptance of Technology

Looking next at measures for technology acceptance, **Figure 12**, immediately below, summarizes wealth and illustrates software market sizes and Internet usage as a percent of the total population for the five largest European economies, plus Benelux and Scandinavia + Finland, sorted by total software market size. The U.S. and Canada are added for reference.

| Country | GDP per Person / Total GDP | # People (million) | Total Software Market | | Internet Users | | |
			2010 Total / Tech Adoption	2010-13 Forecasted Growth	Actual (million)	World Rank	% of People
U.S.	$46,900 $14,630 billion	312	$130.0 bill. advanced	5.4%	240	2	77%
Germany	$35,800 $ 2,930 billion	82	$21.6 billion advanced	8.8%	65	6	80%
UK	$35,300 $ 2,180 billion	62	$21.3 billion advanced	9.5%	51	7	83%

Country	GDP per Person / Total GDP	# People (million)	Total Software Market		Internet Users		
			2010 Total / Tech Adoption	2010-13 Forecasted Growth	Actual (million)	World Rank	% of People
France	$32,600 $ 2,150 billion	66	$15.4 billion advanced	9.5%	45	9	68%
Benelux	$39,800 $ 1,110 billion	28	$12.0 billion advanced	11.5%	23	21	84%
Scandi-navia + Finland	$39,400 $ 1,000 billion	25	$11.1 billion advanced	11.7%	22	22	87%
Italy	$29,200 $ 1,770 billion	61	$10.0 billion advanced	9.6%	30	14	50%
Canada	$38,800 $ 1,330 billion	34	$ 9.8 billion advanced	5.8%	26	12	76%
Spain	$29,300 $ 1,350 billion	46	$ 9.1 billion advanced	11.8%	29	15	63%
TOTAL: Euro. Top 7	$33,800 $12,491 bill.	369	$ 100.6 bill. all advanced	10.1%	266		72%

Figure 12 – EUROPE: GDP, Population, Total Software Markets[x], Internet Usage[xi]

Regarding Internet usage, Benelux and Scandinavia + Finland have some of the highest usage rates in the world; approximately 85% of the population uses the Internet. Norway and Sweden both exceed 90%, the only two sizable countries in the world with this honor. By implication, the acceptance rate for embracing technology is high in these territories. Note also that the UK Internet usage rate is higher than the other large countries of Europe (Germany, France, Spain, and Italy), which implies that technology acceptance is higher in the UK than in these other four large European economies.

Figure 13 shows 2010 total software markets and 2010-2013 forecasted growth rates for Europe, with Canada and the U.S. added for reference. It also shows percentages of regional and world totals:

| Country | 2010 Total Software Market ($ billions) | Software Market % of Total | | 2010 – 2013 Forecasted Growth | 2013 Forecast | |
		% Europe	% World		Total Software Market ($ billions)	% World
U.S.	$130.0	129.2%	40.0%	5.4%	$152.0	37.2%
Germany	$21.6	17.8%	6.6%	8.8%	$27.7	6.8%
UK	$21.3	17.6%	6.6%	9.5%	$28.1	6.8%
France	$15.4	12.7%	4.7%	9.5%	$20.2	4.9%
Benelux	$12.0	9.9%	3.7%	11.5%	$16.6	4.1%
Scandi-navia + Finland	$11.1	9.2%	3.4%	11.7%	$15.5	3.8%
Italy	$10.0	8.3%	3.1%	9.6%	$13.2	3.2%
Canada	$ 9.8	9.7%	3.0%	5.8%	$11.6	2.8%
Spain	$ 9.1	7.5%	2.8%	11.8%	$12.7	3.1%
TOTAL: Europe Top 7	$100.6	82.9%	30.9%	10.1%	$134.1	32.7%

Figure 13 – EUROPE: 2010-2013 Total Software Market Sizes, Growth Rates, % of Total Region & World

Europe's forecasted software market growth for 2010-2013 is much higher than the forecast for the U.S. and Canada; 10.1% for Europe compared to 5.4% and 5.8% respectively for the U.S. and Canada. If this forecasted growth comes to fruition, the top seven countries in Europe will represent one-third of the world's software market by 2013 and total Europe will account for approximately 40% of the world's software market.

Figure 14 illustrates the European software markets graphically, comparing the total software markets by country to GDP PPP by country for the seven largest countries/regions of Europe:

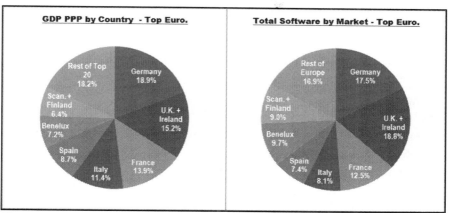

Figure 14 – Top Europe Economies: GDP vs. Total Software Market Sizes

This chart shows graphically how much of the European market can be captured by selling in the top seven countries/regions.

Figure 15 ranks the seven largest countries/regions of Europe for software market intensity: those that have a higher share of total European software than share of total European GDP, and a higher percentage of their GDP's attributable to software sales:

Country	% of Total Europe			Software Sales as % of GDP
	Software Market Size	GDP PPP	Index[xix]	
Scandinavia + Finland	9.0%	6.4%	141	1.35%
Benelux	9.7%	7.2%	135	1.18%
UK + Ireland	18.8%	15.2%	123	2.26%
Germany	17.3%	18.9%	92	0.60%
France	12.5%	13.9%	90	0.53%
Spain	7.4%	8.7%	85	0.60%
Italy	8.1%	11.4%	71	0.44%
Total Europe			100	0.66%

Figure 15 – EUROPE: Comparison of GDP Share to Total Software Market Share

Figure 15, directly above, indicates that the countries that make up Northern Europe (Scandinavia + Finland, Benelux, UK + Ireland) have the highest shares of the total European software market compared to their shares of GDP. They also have a higher share of their GDP attributable to software. Software sales account for over 2% of the UK GDP! This is more than twice the percentage of software sales in the U.S. economy, which is 0.88% of GDP. The UK appears to be the highest in the world on this measure.

Another approach to assessing technology acceptance across countries is the World Economic Forum's network readiness index (NRI), which was described in detail directly before **Figure 7** on page 20 and a custom index to measure "readiness to embrace to enterprise software" on the same scale: 1 (low) to 7 (high). Illustrated in **Figure 16** below are the NRI and custom index results for Europe and other selected countries:

	NRI Index					Custom Index: Enterprise Software (Scale of 1 to 7, low to high)							
						12.5%	22.5%	12.5%	15.0%	12.5%	25.0%	100%	
	Index Score (1 - 7, LO - Hi)	World Rank: '10-'11	Change: '10→'11	World Rank: '06-'07	Change: '07→'11	Avail. Of Latest Tech.	Laws Relating to ICT	Avail. - Scientists & Eng.	Buyer Sophistication	Extent of Staff Training	Co. Level of Tech. Absorp.	CUSTOM INDEX	CUSTOM INDEX, U.K. = 100
Europe													
Sweden	5.60	1	0	2	1	6.8	5.9	5.8	5.0	5.7	6.4	5.97	112
Norway	5.21	9	1	10	1	6.7	5.6	5.1	4.5	5.5	6.2	5.65	106
Finland	5.43	3	3	4	1	6.6	5.5	6.0	4.4	5.2	6.0	5.62	106
Denmark	5.29	7	-4	1	-6	6.4	5.7	5.1	4.3	5.4	6.0	5.54	104
Germany	5.14	13	1	16	3	6.3	5.3	4.8	4.4	5.2	6.0	5.39	101
Netherlands	5.19	11	-2	6	-5	6.4	5.3	5.0	4.6	5.1	5.6	5.35	101
U.K.	5.12	15	-2	9	-6	6.4	5.4	4.8	4.6	4.7	5.7	5.32	100
France	4.92	20	-2	23	3	6.4	5.2	5.3	4.1	4.7	5.6	5.24	98
Belgium	4.80	23	-1	24	1	6.4	4.9	5.3	4.4	4.9	5.5	5.21	98
Spain	4.33	37	-3	32	-5	5.8	4.5	4.4	3.8	3.7	5.2	4.62	87
Italy	3.97	51	-3	38	-13	5.0	4.0	4.3	4.0	3.2	4.3	4.14	78
Selected Other Countries													
U.S.	5.33	5	0	7	2	6.4	5.4	5.7	4.5	5.1	6.0	5.54	104
Canada	5.21	8	-1	11	3	6.4	5.5	5.6	4.7	5.0	5.6	5.47	103
Australia	5.06	17	-1	15	-2	6.1	5.5	4.5	4.4	4.8	5.9	5.30	100
Japan	4.95	19	2	14	-5	6.3	4.7	5.8	5.2	5.4	6.3	5.60	105
S. Korea	5.19	10	5	19	9	6.1	5.1	4.9	4.6	4.4	6.1	5.29	99
Brazil	3.90	56	5	53	-3	5.5	4.5	4.0	3.6	4.2	5.2	4.57	86
India	4.03	48	-5	44	-4	5.6	4.5	5.2	3.8	4.1	5.3	4.77	80
China	4.35	36	1	59	23	4.4	4.4	4.6	4.6	4.1	4.9	4.54	76
Indonesia	3.92	53	14	62	9	4.8	3.9	4.7	3.9	4.4	4.9	4.43	74

Figure 16 – EUROPE: NRI and Custom Enterprise Software Readiness Index

As might be expected, the European countries discussed above as being the best for technology acceptance have the top rankings in the "readiness to embrace enterprise software" custom index: Sweden, Norway, Finland, and Denmark. These are followed in a lower tier by Germany, France, and the UK, along with the smaller countries of Netherlands and Belgium. Spain and Italy are in a lower tier yet, and their NRI and custom software indices are nearer to other countries such as India, China, and Brazil. Finland and the Scandinavian countries have the highest NRIs in the world, with Sweden and Finland ranked first and third and all of the others in the top ten.

The high performance of Finland and the Scandinavian countries are attributable to their governments implementing sound planning, high Internet usage by individuals and businesses, effective educational systems, and a wide swath of public and private organizations accepting technology and using it to optimize their business processes.

Europe: Summary of Wealth and Acceptance of Technology

To summarize the *Wealth* and *Acceptance of Technology* section, the best markets for enterprise software vendors in Europe are the top five economies of Germany, France, UK + Ireland, Italy, and Spain and the two artificial regions of Scandinavia + Finland and Benelux, which all together account for 80% of Europe's total GDP PPP.

The GDP per person for these seven territories can be categorized as:

- **Scandinavia + Finland, Benelux**
  The top of the *Wealthy* range at almost US $40,000.

- **Germany, UK + Ireland, France**
  The middle of the *Wealthy* range around $35,000.

- **Spain, Italy**
  The bottom of the *Wealthy* range, near or slightly below $30,000.

Regarding technology acceptance as measured by total software markets and Internet usage, the UK, Scandinavia + Finland, and Benelux have some of the highest technology usage and adoption rates in the world, with the remaining four large European countries still high in worldwide terms, but slightly lower than the first three.

Europe: Acceptance of English as a Language for Commerce

English as the language for commerce is crucial when considering market entry for enterprise software sales, because it is by far the most widely spoken language in the technology world. Assuming that most enterprise software is initially written in English, many start their international expansion in English-speaking countries and those where English is widely used and understood in the business world. This enables the cost for translating the software into other languages to be deferred and allows a software vendor to gain international field experience to better understand the required order of other languages.

Examining the top European countries with regards to both the *Wealth* and *Acceptance of Technology* dimensions, here are the primary languages of business commerce:

- **UK + Ireland**
  English (with regard to the U.S.: "two countries separated by a common language").

- **Germany**
  German, except for limited software in large data centers, enterprise software products cannot be sold without German translation. Web sites and marketing material need to be translated into German as well.

- **France**
  French, except for limited software in large data centers, enterprise software products cannot be sold without French translation. Web sites and marketing material need to be translated into French as well. The French sometimes resist things considered too American or too British. With a dismissive wave of the hand, the French mutter "too Anglo-Saxon."

- **Italy**
  Italian, except for limited software in large data centers, enterprise software products cannot be sold without Italian translation. Web sites and marketing material need to be translated into Italian.

- **Spain**

Spanish, except for limited software in large data centers, enterprise software products cannot be sold without Spanish translation. Web sites and marketing material need to be translated into Spanish as well. There is less English spoken among business professionals here than in the other four large European markets.

- **Benelux (Belgium, Netherlands, and Luxembourg)**
  - **Belgium**
    - ◆ Flemish (the majority) – Dutch.
    - ◆ Walloons – Mostly French, but also some German.
    - ◆ Brussels Capital Region – Officially bilingual Dutch and French, however the native language of the majority is French. EU headquarters are located here, with many thousands employed to support EU headquarters. This is similar to the large number of Washington DC's federal government employees.
  - **Netherlands –** Dutch.
  - **Luxembourg –** Trilingual German, French, and Luxembourgish. Remember that Luxembourg has the second highest GDP PPP per person in the world at US $80,300 for its small population of 500,000.

Because there are so many languages spoken in the countries that make up Benelux, many technology professionals speak English fluently, in addition to two or three other languages. For the first stage of market entry, most enterprise software products would probably be adequate in English across Benelux. For this stage of market development, web sites and marketing material can be in English. To gain market traction to evolve local sales operations, products, web sites, and marketing materials translated into German and French would increase the chances for success.

- **Scandinavia + Finland**

Each country has its own native language. However, the population of these countries is so small that most people speak a few other Scandinavian languages, as well as being fluent in English.

In these countries, most technology professionals speak English fluently, in addition to several other languages. An enterprise software product in English will probably be adequate across Scandinavia +

Finland for all stages. Web sites and marketing material can also be in English.

Europe: The Technology Sales and Buying Culture

As described above, this measurement is based on the similarity of the market's technology evaluation and buying practices to those of the U.S. and Canada. These territories, along with the large European countries, are chosen as benchmarks because they are the dominant markets for enterprise software. Additionally, part of assessing the *Technology Sales and Buying Culture* dimension is the all-important availability of qualified people to staff international sales operation start-up. The most important functions at the outset are:

1. **Sales Staff** – Those who can sell directly as well as manage sales through channels.

2. **Technical Staff** – Those having strong people skills for presales support, for training channel partners, and having the technical knowledge to drive consultative sales.

The following sections present the European countries/regions in order from most similar to North America to most dissimilar.

1. UK and Ireland – *Advanced* Technology Adoption

In Europe, the most similar buying culture to North America is the UK + Ireland. One of the major contributing factors is the presence of many large multinationals in these countries.

- **The UK in General**
  Its native English language, heritage as the "mother country" of the U.S., and its laws that make it easy for companies to set up their European headquarters are a few reasons why the UK is a prime location for multinationals. It is within the EU but viewed as a less foreign culture than continental Europe.

- **London**
  Many consider London to be one of the top financial capitals of the world.

  London is ranked number one in the Global Financial Centres Index, the World's Most Economically Powerful City, and the

Worldwide Centres of Commerce Index[xx]. London is also the leading foreign currency exchange center; one of the top cities for trading operations in financial assets, energy, and commodities; and a major center for international and investment banking.

As a Global City[xxi], London is ranked number two in the Global Cities Index, Global Power City Index, and the World City Survey, just behind New York in all three surveys. Incidentally, Tokyo and Paris rank third and fourth, respectively, in each of these surveys.

The UK has an ideal time zone that can connect to almost anywhere in the world during the business day. Also, London has the highest number of international flights of any city in the world from its three international airports.

- **Ireland**

  Despite its battle with the financial meltdown that started in 2009, Ireland is the leading center for technology company call centers in Europe. During its boom years from approximately 2000–2008, many Eastern Europeans flocked here because of its booming economy, resulting in a wide variety of languages being spoken in Ireland.

With a compelling business case, medium-sized and enterprise organizations in the UK are willing to take risks on new software technologies, with the same openness as organizations in the U.S. Though the data is not completely reliable, the UK's SaaS market is approximately the same size as Germany's, the largest in Europe and the third largest SaaS market in the world behind the U.S. and Japan.

The UK + Ireland have an excellent supply of English-speaking software sales and technical people, because many software vendors have started up and built their European operations here. Some might even speak other European languages, such as Spanish, French, or German, and maybe even an Asian language. A competent enterprise software salesperson usually has the same personality type as a strong salesperson in the U.S., which enables North American sales management staff to recognize and assess them easily.

Unfortunately, the compensation costs for these talented sales and technical people in the UK + Ireland is high compared to North America, due to the high cost of living and the demand from other technology companies. Compared to other parts of Europe, the employer taxes, number of statutory vacation/holiday days, and other overhead costs (called "social costs" in Europe) are lower in the UK + Ireland, although high by comparison to the U.S. Also, it is less difficult to downsize when necessary in the UK + Ireland than in the rest of Europe. In other parts of Europe, it is costly to terminate employees if a company needs to be shuttered or shrunk. The result is that many software entrepreneurs go outside Europe to start up their companies.

To get a sense for the best industry segments for enterprise software vendors to target in the UK, **Figure 17** shows the breakdown of total technology spending by vertical segment for the UK, with comparison to Total Europe, UK, Benelux and Scandinavia + Finland:

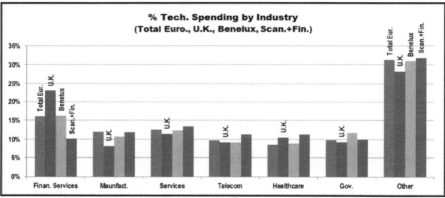

Figure 17 – Total Technology Spending[xxii] by Leading Industry Segments: UK, Benelux, Scandinavia + Finland

The UK's financial services industry sector has outsized technology spending compared to the rest of Northern Europe and the other European countries. Other than this difference and a slightly lower percentage spent on the manufacturing sector, the UK's spending by sector is similar to Total Europe, Benelux, and Scandinavia + Finland.

2. Scandinavia + Finland and Benelux – Advanced Technology Adoption

The next most desirable locales for enterprise software market entry after UK + Ireland are Scandinavia + Finland (Norway, Denmark, Sweden, Finland) and Benelux (Belgium, Netherlands, Luxembourg). In both of these regions, buying behavior in target organizations for enterprise software is similar to the UK + Ireland, although decision-makers are more hesitant to embrace new technology. There is also a good supply of large multi-nationals; however, less than in the UK + Ireland. The availability of English-speaking staff with enterprise software experience is plentiful, but technicians are harder to find in both regions than in UK + Ireland. Although English-speaking skills are widespread across both regions, there are more fluent English-speakers in Scandinavia + Finland than in Benelux. Sales talent will be recognizable to U.S. international sales management staff in both regions, but sales personalities tend to be lower key than many top U.S. enterprise software sales reps seem to be. Enterprise software technology skills might be slightly more widespread in Benelux than in Scandinavia + Finland.

Compensation costs and social costs are higher in both of these regions than in UK + Ireland. Statutory rules for four weeks or more of vacation are widespread within the seven countries that make up these two regions. Very strict laws for termination, especially in Scandinavia + Finland, drive up employment costs.

All in all, Scandinavia + Finland and Benelux are high on the priority list for market entry of enterprise software vendors in Europe.

See **Figure 17** on page 38, for the breakdown of total technology spending by leading industry segments for Benelux and Scandinavia + Finland compared to the UK and Total Europe. Other than Scandinavia + Finland having lower technology spending in the financial services segment, both regions have comparable spending by industry segment to each other, and to the UK and Total Europe.

3. Germany and France – *Advanced* Technology Adoption

After UK + Ireland, Scandinavia + Finland, and Benelux comes Germany and France, the original drivers behind the creation of the EU. These countries are large and proud of their heritage and cultures, which differentiates Germany and France's business cultures and buying behavior from North America and the other European regions described so far. Locals are required for selling and supporting enterprise software, and the challenge for market entry is finding locals who are fluent English-speakers along with their native German or French. The competition for such staff, both for sales and technical, increases compensation costs. It is difficult for an American to recognize sales talent because of the cultural differences. The cultural gap is wide enough that local German and French management's understanding of business cultures must span North America and their own. However, local managers such as this earn high compensation. There is additional risk that if a local manager is hired and then is not effective, strict labor laws make it very difficult to terminate their contract. Many enterprise software vendors have made costly mistakes in staffing local sales management in Germany and France, which is not only expensive to fix, but can set back market expansion for years.

There is also some degree of anti-American sentiment in France. This is a complicated issue that stems from French insecurity about their culture being overwhelmed by American culture.

Germany and France have some of the highest social costs in the world. Laws governing statutory vacation, shortened work weeks, and termination are heavily slanted toward the German or French employee to the detriment of the employer. However, the countries are large enough that German and French medium and enterprise companies expect local salespeople and local support.

Despite these difficulties, Germany and France are large, rich markets that have high tech acceptance and together account for almost one-third of total European GDP PPP. However, it is usually preferable to expand into these countries after gaining experience in the friendlier and more accommodating Northern European markets described above.

To measure the top industry segments for enterprise software vendors to target in Germany and France, **Figure 18** indicates the breakdown of total technology spending by vertical segment for Germany and France, with comparisons to Total Europe and the UK:

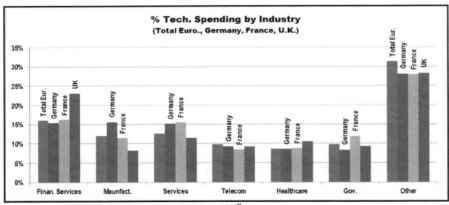

Figure 18 – Total Technology Spending[xxii] by Leading Industry Segments: Germany, France, UK

The only segments that vary much from Total Europe and the UK are Germany's higher spending on manufacturing and France's slightly higher spending on government, neither of which is surprising.

4. Spain and Italy – *Advanced* Technology Adoption

These are the larger markets of southern Europe, whose markets and technology cultures are even more dissimilar to North America than those of Germany and France. The business climate is much more casual in Spain and Italy than in Northern Europe. The weather is warm, meals are unhurried; many in Spain still leave the office for two hours midday for napping at home (siestas). Both economies shut down for six weeks in the summer, when almost everyone takes vacation at the same time. Predicting when enterprise software deals will close is challenging, and no enterprise software purchase decisions will be made from the end of June until early September. In these business environments, it is very difficult for an outsider to determine who will succeed in sales or whether staff is working hard enough.

In addition to their cultural dissimilarities, Spain and Italy have smaller economies than the other three large European economies (approximately two-thirds as large) and they have lower wealth. GDP per person is at the top of the *Upper Middle Income* instead of the *Wealthy* range. The composition of GDP, especially in Italy, is skewed much more toward smaller businesses.

With business environments such as these, it is obvious that Spanish and Italian sales operations are usually established after Northern Europe, Germany, and France. These are great places for vacation, but challenging places in which to do business.

To quantify the top industry segments for enterprise software vendors to target in Spain and Italy, **Figure 19** illustrates technology spending by vertical segment for Spain and Italy, with comparisons to Total Europe and the UK:

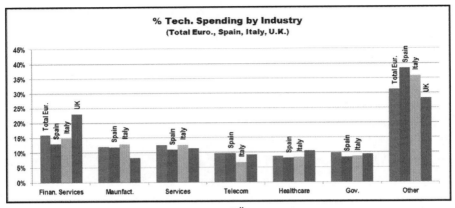

Figure 19 – Total Technology Spending[xxii] by Leading Industry Segments: Spain, Italy, UK

No segments for total technology spending in Spain and Italy vary much from Total Europe and the UK.

5. The Rest of Europe – *Basic* and *Mid-Level* Technology Adoption

Outside the top four economies of Europe and the three contrived regions of UK + Ireland, Scandinavia + Finland, and Benelux, there are 28 smaller countries with GDP PPPs totaling approximately 20% of total Europe GDP. The combined population of these countries is 186 million—almost one-third of Europe's total population. However, this fragmented territory is poor (two-thirds of GDP per person compared to Europe as a whole), has fewer medium and enterprise companies for target markets, has lower technology acceptance, has different buying practices, and has a weak supply of potential enterprise software sales and tech staff. This area is the last destination for enterprise software vendors.

When an enterprise software vendor has international sales operations in the seven more desirable European countries/regions and wants to gain access to this last 20% of Europe, a typical model would be a few regional sales offices supported by channels in most of these small countries.

Europe: Summary – Results from 4 Dimensions of Country Evaluation

Figure 20, immediately below, summarizes the 4 Dimensions of Country Evaluation for Europe. Note that Canada and Australia/New Zealand are included for comparison (currency used is U.S. $):

Country / Region	GDP Category & US$ GDP Per Person	# People	Total Software Market		2010-13 Forecasted Growth	English for Language of Commerce?	Tech Sales & Buying Culture
			2010 ($ billion)	Tech. Adoption			
UK + Ireland	Wealthy $35,500	66.3 million	$21.3 advanced		9.5%	Yes – native speakers	• Most similar in Europe to N. America in buying and business culture • Strong supply of sales & tech talent • Higher compensation & employment costs than U.S.
Benelux	Top Wealthy $39,800	27.9 million	$12.0 advanced		11.5%	Yes for Netherlands; most cases OK for Belgium & Luxembourg	• Somewhat similar buying behavior to N. America • Reasonable supply of sales & tech talent; must pay a premium for English fluency • Very high compensation & employment costs
Scandi-navia + Finland	Top Wealthy $39,400	25.3 million	$11.1 advanced		11.7%	Yes	• Somewhat similar buying behavior to N. America • Reasonable supply of sales & tech talent, must pay a premium for strong tech talent • Very high compensation & employment costs

Country / Region	GDP Category & US$ GDP Per Person	# People	Total Software Market			English for Language of Commerce?	Tech Sales & Buying Culture
			2010 ($ billion) – Tech. Adoption	2010-13 Forecasted Growth			
Germany	Wealthy $35,800	81.8 million	$21.6 advanced	8.8%	No	• Dissimilar business culture to N. America • Medium supply of sales & tech talent; difficult for U.S. manager to recognize talent • Must pay a premium for local manager to bridge German and N. American culture • High compensation & very high employment costs
France	Wealthy $32,600	65.8 million	$15.4 advanced	9.5%	No	• Dissimilar business culture to U.S.; some anti-American sentiment • Medium supply of sales & tech talent; difficult for U.S. manager to recognize talent • Must pay a premium for local manager to bridge French and N. American culture • High compensation & very high employment costs
Italy	Top Upper Middle Income $29,200	60.6 million	$10.0 advanced	9.6%	No	• Very dissimilar business culture to N. America; sometimes viewed as too relaxed and disorganized by N. American business standards • Buying behavior and decision-making radically different than N. America

Country / Region	GDP Category & US$ GDP Per Person	# People	Total Software Market			English for Language of Commerce?	Tech Sales & Buying Culture
			2010 ($ billion) — Tech. Adoption		2010-13 Forecasted Growth		
Spain	Top Upper Middle Income $29,300	46.2 million	$9.1 advanced		11.8%	No	• Very dissimilar business culture to N. America; sometimes viewed as too relaxed and disorganized by N. American business standards • Buying behavior and decision-making radically different than N. America
Rest of Europe	Middle Income $18,800	186 million	$20.8 mid-level		11.0%	Mostly no, except for small pockets	28 small countries best suited for regional offices and channel sales
Australia + New Zealand	Wealthy $37,100	27.0 million	$4.4 advanced		7.0%	Yes – native	• Other than Canada, most similar to N. America in buying and business culture • Strong supply of sales & tech talent; developed, self-sufficient tech culture because of geographic isolation • Comparable compensation & higher employment costs than U.S.
Canada	Wealthy $38,800	34.3 million	$9.8 advanced		5.8%	Yes, except for Quebec with French	• Very close to U.S. in buying culture and similar business culture • Strong supply of sales & tech talent • Comparable comp. & higher employment costs than U.S.

Figure 20 – EUROPE: Summary of 4 Dimensions for Country Evaluation

Putting it All Together for Europe

Taking all 4 Dimensions into account illustrates why most enterprise software vendors start their European sales expansion in Northern Europe, and many start in the UK + Ireland.

Once sales have commenced in Northern Europe, the next areas for expansion are usually Germany and France. Market entry into Germany and France requires investment:

1. For local managers who can bridge cultures and translate business issues between North America and Germany/France

2. The expense of forming French and German subsidiaries, which are advantageous for employing staff in these countries

3. The expense of translating software, web and marketing materials into German and French to initiate sales in these countries

The last on the list of desirable territories for enterprise software are Spain and Italy. Smaller market potential for enterprise software and radically different business cultures place these locations lower on the priority list for international expansion for a typical enterprise software vendor.

4 EAST ASIA

Introduction

The geographic boundaries of East Asia, as defined in this book, create a rough rectangle several thousand miles on each side:

1. Southwest: India
2. Northwest: China
3. Northeast: Japan and South Korea
4. Southeast: Indonesia

Figure 21, a map of East Asia, follows:

East Asia

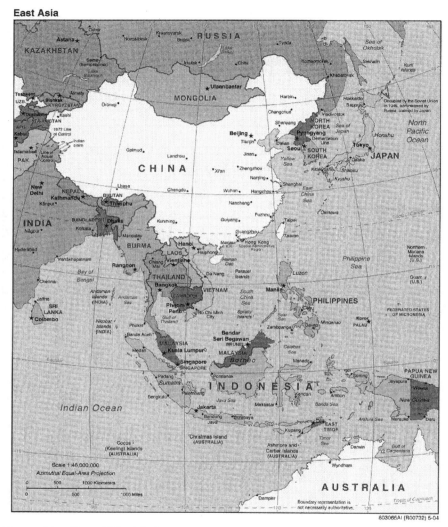

803066AI (R00732) 5-04

Figure 21 – Map of East Asia

Australia and New Zealand are considered separately from East Asia. See Chapter 6, starting on page 113.

Of all the regions of the world, East Asia is the most diverse in terms of geography, country size, and business culture. It is by far the most populous area in the world with slightly more than half of the world's population. It now accounts for one-third of the world's GDP in PPP terms. Compare this to the worldwide share of the U.S. and the European Union at approximately 20% each. East Asia's share of the world's GDP is increasing, as the U.S. and European economies are growing slowly, if at all. By contrast, all the East Asian countries (with the exception of Japan and Thailand) are experiencing rapid growth. They did not even pause during the economic crash of 2008–2009.

The challenge for enterprise software vendors considering East Asia is that few generalizations are possible across the entire region, and each of the 4 major areas must be considered separately, as **Figure 22** illustrates:

Total GDP Rank		GDP using PPP (US $ billions)				Population (millions)				GDP (PPP) / Person		
		World Rank	US$ (billion)	% of E. Asia	% of World	World Rank	People (millions)	% of E. Asia	% of World	US $	E. Asia Rank	Index (E. Asia x 100)
1. Greater China												
	China (includes Hong Kong)	2	10,084	40.9%	13.6%	1	1,342.5	36.2%	19.5%	7,511	8	113
	Taiwan	19	820	3.3%	1.1%	49	23.1	0.6%	0.3%	35,498	3	534
TOTAL - Greater China			$ 10,904	44.2%	14.7%		1,365.6	36.8%	19.8%	$ 7,985		120
2. India		4	$ 4,001	16.2%	5.4%		1,194.4	32.2%	17.3%	$ 3,350		50
3. Japan / Korea												
	Japan	3	4,309	17.5%	5.8%	10	127.3	3.4%	1.8%	33,849	4	509
	S. Korea	12	1,457	5.9%	2.0%	26	48.5	1.3%	0.7%	30,041	5	452
TOTAL - Japan / Korea			$ 5,766	23.4%	7.8%		175.8	4.7%	2.5%	$ 32,799		493
4. SE Asia												
	Indonesia	15	1,027	4.2%	1.4%	4	237.6	6.4%	3.4%	4,322	9	65
	Thailand	24	585	2.4%	0.8%	20	67.1	1.8%	1.0%	8,718	7	131
	Malaysia	29	412	1.7%	0.6%	45	27.6	0.7%	0.4%	14,928	6	224
	Philippines	33	350	1.4%	0.5%	12	94.0	2.5%	1.4%	3,723	10	56
	Singapore	39	291	1.2%	0.4%	115	5.1	0.1%	0.1%	57,059	1	858
TOTAL - SE Asia			$ 2,665	10.8%	3.6%		431.4	11.6%	6.3%	$ 6,178		93

Figure 22 – GDP & Population: Four Major Regions of East Asia

And graphically, in **Figure 23**:

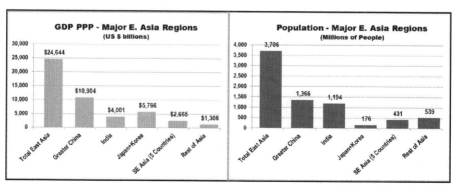

Figure 23 – GDP & Population Graphs: East Asia Regions

The data from **Figure 23** highlights some of the contrasts of the four East Asian regions:

1. Each has markedly different populations, total GDP PPP, and GDP PPP per person
2. Each has a distinct business culture
3. Each is at a different stage of economic development
4. Each has radically different assortments of local medium-sized and enterprise organizations that are the targets for enterprise software
5. All are far apart geographically

The technology sales and buying culture for each region are radically different from the U.S. and Europe as well, each having its own unique aspects. Another characteristic of East Asian countries is their hostility toward each other, although this doesn't prevent them from doing business with one another. However, this does affect where to locate regional sales offices to support the countries. For example, South Korea and Japan cannot be supported by a single office in either country, because Japan occupied Korea most recently from 1910–1945. This has engendered hostility from South Koreans toward the Japanese, especially older citizens.

These contrasts present a significant challenge for enterprise software vendors considering expansion into East Asia, because there is no typical formula or order for market entry. This contrasts starkly with both Europe and Latin America, which have an order for typical enterprise software vendor market entry.

Despite the challenges of entering the East Asian markets, this part of the world is crucial for software vendors. The continued rapid economic growth in eight of the ten countries listed in **Figure 22**, above, signifies the influence and economic might of East Asian countries is rapidly increasing and will be for the foreseeable future. Only Japan and Thailand are exceptions to the growth dynamics. And although Japan presents significant challenges including economic malaise, recent natural disasters, and high entry barriers, it is the third largest economy and sixth largest software market in the world.

East Asia: Wealth

Figure 24 shows the 2010 GDP PPP and population data for the top thirteen East Asian economies ranked by total GDP PPP. The gray stripes are for ease of reading and have no other significance.

GDP Rank		GDP using PPP (US $ billions)				Population (millions)				GDP (PPP) / Person (calculated)		
	World Rank	US$ (billion)	% of Asia	% of World	World Rank	People (millions)	% of Asia	% of World		US $	Rank On List	Index (East Asia =100)
1. China	2	10,084	40.9%	13.6%	1	1,342.5	36.2%	19.5%		7,511	8	113
2. Japan	3	4,309	17.5%	5.8%	10	127.3	3.4%	1.8%		33,849	4	509
3. India	4	4,001	16.2%	5.4%	2	1,194.4	32.2%	17.3%		3,350	11	50
4. S. Korea	12	1,457	5.9%	2.0%	26	48.5	1.3%	0.7%		30,041	5	452
5. Indonesia	15	1,027	4.2%	1.4%	4	237.6	6.4%	3.4%		4,322	9	65
6. Taiwan	19	820	3.3%	1.1%	49	23.1	0.6%	0.3%		35,498	3	534
7. Thailand	24	585	2.4%	0.8%	20	67.1	1.8%	1.0%		8,718	7	131
8. Pakistan	27	465	1.9%	0.6%	6	171.9	4.6%	2.5%		2,705	13	41
9. Malaysia	29	412	1.7%	0.6%	45	27.6	0.7%	0.4%		14,928	6	224
10. Philippines	33	350	1.4%	0.5%	12	94.0	2.5%	1.4%		3,723	10	56
11. Hong Kong		322	1.3%	0.4%		7.1	0.2%	0.1%		45,352	2	682
12. Singapore	39	291	1.2%	0.4%	115	5.1	0.1%	0.1%		57,059	1	858
13. Vietnam	40	276	1.1%	0.4%	13	86.9	2.3%	1.3%		3,176	12	48
TOTAL - East Asia		$ 24,644		33.3%		3,706		53.7%		$ 6,650		100

Figure 24 – EAST ASIA: Top 13 Economies Ranked by 2010 GDP[xxiii]

Ranked by size of economy, China, Japan, and India dominate East Asia with their combined GDP encompassing 75% of the East Asian total and their combined population 72% of the total. The Chinese and Indian economies are forecasted to continue growing at the annual rate of 8%–10% in the medium term, but both economies are showing signs of overheating with inflation, over-taxed infrastructure, and, for China, possibly a real estate asset bubble. The Chinese government has also announced a shift from a focus on increasing exports to concentrating on internal consumption, but it remains to be seen if this really will change. Japan, although one of the most advanced economies in the world, has had little economic growth since its asset bubble popped twenty years ago. Japanese confidence has waned since China took over its place as the second largest economy in the world, as expressed in current exchange-rate terms[xxiv]. Also contributing to the lack of confidence and slackening consumer demand is Japan's relentless deflation and the beginnings of a population decline unprecedented in modern history. At its current birth rates, Japan's population is forecasted to decline 30% over the next 30 years. In contract to Japan, South Korea is exhibiting rapid growth and development. South Korean multinationals are showing great success in major worldwide industries such as consumer electronics (Samsung, LG) and automobiles (Hyundai). However, South Korea is under constant military threat by its belligerent and unstable neighbor, North Korea. Seoul, the capital of South Korea, is barely thirty miles from the border with North Korea. Indonesia is another interesting economy. It is rapidly developing, now the fourth most populous country in the world, and a much better place in which to do business than ever before.

To summarize, East Asia is experiencing rapid growth because most of its major economies are expanding, from the huge countries of China and India; medium-sized South Korea, Indonesia, Malaysia, and Taiwan; still developing Vietnam and Philippines; and tiny Singapore and Hong Kong. The only exceptions are Japan and Thailand.

Figure 25 ranks the countries of East Asia by GDP PPP per person. The gray stripes are significant, as they delineate the categories of GDP per person as described in **Figure 4** on page 14:

GDP Rank		GDP using PPP (US $ billions)				Population (millions)				GDP (PPP) / Person (calculated)		
		World Rank	US$ (billion)	% of Asia	% of World	World Rank	People (millions)	% of Asia	% of World	US $	Rank On List	Index (East Asia =100)
12.	Singapore	39	291	1.2%	0.4%	115	5.1	0.1%	0.1%	57,059	1	858
11.	Hong Kong		322	1.3%	0.4%		7.1	0.2%	0.1%	45,352	2	682
6.	Taiwan	19	820	3.3%	1.1%	49	23.1	0.6%	0.3%	35,498	3	534
2.	Japan	3	4,309	17.5%	5.8%	10	127.3	3.4%	1.8%	33,849	4	509
4.	S. Korea	12	1,457	5.9%	2.0%	26	48.5	1.3%	0.7%	30,041	5	452
9.	Malaysia	29	412	1.7%	0.6%	45	27.6	0.7%	0.4%	14,928	6	224
7.	Thailand	24	585	2.4%	0.8%	20	67.1	1.8%	1.0%	8,718	7	131
1.	China	2	10,084	40.9%	13.6%	1	1,342.5	36.2%	19.5%	7,511	8	113
5.	Indonesia	15	1,027	4.2%	1.4%	4	237.6	6.4%	3.4%	4,322	9	65
10.	Philippines	33	350	1.4%	0.5%	12	94.0	2.5%	1.4%	3,723	10	56
3.	India	4	4,001	16.2%	5.4%	2	1,194.4	32.2%	17.3%	3,350	11	50
13.	Vietnam	40	276	1.1%	0.4%	13	86.9	2.3%	1.3%	3,176	12	48
8.	Pakistan	27	465	1.9%	0.6%	6	171.9	4.6%	2.5%	2,705	13	41
TOTAL - East Asia			$ 24,644		33.3%		3,706		53.7%	$ 6,650		100

Figure 25 – EAST ASIA: GDP per Person, Ranked from Highest to Lowest

The following sections assess the East Asian countries from highest to lowest GDPs per person:

1. Singapore, Hong Kong – Tiny *Top* and *Wealthy*

These two areas are among the countries with the highest GDPs per person in the world. Singapore is third, and if Hong Kong was a separate country, it would be seventh, right behind the U.S. Despite these impressive numbers, both have very small populations of five and seven million respectively, each approximately the population of the Dallas-Ft. Worth metro area.

Hong Kong is a "special administrative region" of China, given back by the UK in 1997. Its political system and laws are distinct from Mainland China, and its legal system is similar to that of the UK. It has limited autonomy from China, which *does not* include:

- Free election of its leader (who is appointed by China)
- Defense
- Foreign relations

Hong Kong has been one of the most successful economic growth stories in the world, with a business culture that is a unique mix of Chinese entrepreneurialism and English order. It boasts one of the lowest tax rates in the world and is among the freest economies, ranked first for fifteen years by the Index of Economic Freedom[xxv]. No one knows if China will change Hong Kong in the future, but China probably won't make radical changes, because Hong Kong is so successful and profitable to China. However, the Chinese central government has sent unmistakable signals that Shanghai has supplanted Hong Kong as the business capital of China with large investments in infrastructure and increased publicity.

Both Hong Kong and Singapore are the South Asian headquarters for many multinational companies. Consequently, their enterprise software markets are much larger than their small populations might indicate. Hong Kong has been especially dominant in financial services for many years, and although still strong, its influence has been waning as many businesses have moved their headquarters to Shanghai and Beijing within China and to Singapore to take advantage of their secure future, English-speaking culture, and laws friendly to western companies.

2. Taiwan, Japan, South Korea – *Wealthy*

The economic prospects of Taiwan and South Korea are increasing, which are both developing and expanding rapidly. However, both are under political/military clouds: South Korea from North Korea, as outlined above;

and Taiwan, claimed by China as a wayward territory, despite breaking away and forming an independent democratic government in 1949. Regardless of the historical tensions between China and Taiwan, business ties and investment money flowing between Taiwan and China are increasing. Direct business and tourism flights between the two countries have become frequent.

Taiwan has already passed stagnant Japan in GDP per person, and South Korea is expected to surpass Japan as well in the next several years.

Japan seems to have lost its direction after the economic miracle that emerged from its re-building after World War II until the 1990s. Since then, a real estate asset bubble has popped and its economy has barely grown in the last two decades. The entire country is demoralized after being confronted with a series of significant problems:

- Bouts with deflation from which recovery has been very difficult. Spending and investing will not increase from depressed levels if buyers and investors expect prices to be lower in the future.

- The beginning of an unprecedented population decline. The Japanese birth rate has slowed dramatically, and no significant immigration is allowed.

- The natural disasters of the March 2011 earthquake and subsequent tsunami.

- Indecisive political leadership, as government after government fails and is replaced.

Despite the malaise that has continued since the early 1990s, Japan still has the third largest economy in the world.

3. Thailand, Malaysia – Medium-Sized *Developing* and *Middle Income*

Both of these countries are rich in natural resources, a rarity for East Asia. Malaysia is slowly trying to modernize by changing its policies, with some success. However, it is hobbled by the legacy of preservation of native Malay rights in the business world, both in ownership of companies and a reserved number of slots for Malays in large organizations and businesses. Thailand's economy, which had long been one of the most stable business environments in the region, has stagnated as the government has stumbled from one crisis to another and the military has intervened, disturbing the electoral process and threatening its democracy.

4. China, India – Large *Developing*

These are huge countries that could be considered subcontinents. Each is still a developing country but expanding and modernizing rapidly. Both are unique because of their size, business practices, ancient cultures and thousands of years of entrepreneurialism. Despite their huge potential, they are challenging markets for enterprise software vendors. Those challenges will be outlined in the following sections.

5. Indonesia, Philippines, Vietnam – Small to Medium-Sized *Developing*

These are the least developed countries in this group. They have large populations and high potential to develop significantly in the future, but they are not advanced enough—developmentally or technologically—to support large markets for enterprise software.

East Asia: Acceptance of Technology

Levels of acceptance of technology across East Asia vary, which is a common theme for this part of the world because of the huge differences between and within regions. Despite this diversity, which has been illustrated repeatedly in this book, acceptance of technology correlates well to the level of development and wealth. Consumer electronics and cell phones are very advanced across many countries in Asia, but this doesn't always translate into large potential enterprise software markets.

The best way to assess technology acceptance in East Asia is to analyze each of the four major regions that were outlined in **Figure 22 – GDP & Population: Four Major Regions of East Asia**, on page 49.

1. Japan and South Korea – *Advanced* Technology Adoption

Geographically close to each other in northeast Asia, both countries are advanced economies with high technology acceptance in both their consumer and business markets.

Japan – Although it is the most technologically advanced country in Asia, its woes and declining self-confidence as described above are holding back growth. Nevertheless, Japan has world-class enterprise and multinational companies, especially in heavy manufacturing and consumer electronics, and some of the largest banks and other financial institutions in the world. The businesses in these industries invest heavily in technology to increase their productivity, resulting in a high level of technology acceptance and usage.

South Korea – This country has the fastest average Internet connection speed in the world at almost forty mbps. All sizes of businesses are expanding in South Korea: start-ups, medium-sized, and enterprise multinationals including Samsung and Hyundai. These companies, along with many South Korean enterprise businesses, are owned by large conglomerates called "chaebols," some owning fifty or more companies. Chaebols differ from the Japanese version of business conglomerates, keiretsu, because the chaebol owns 100% of its businesses, rather than the companies having cross-ownership stakes in each other. Technology purchase decisions are generally not made centrally in chaebols, but they can recommend technology investments to other member companies. This tendency is advantageous for enterprise software vendors and increases the level of tech acceptance in chaebols and across the South Korean economy for medium and enterprise business and organizations.

2. Small Countries of Southeast Asia

- **Singapore** – *Advanced* Technology Adoption
- **Malaysia and Thailand** – *Mid-Level* Technology Adoption
- **Philippines and Indonesia** – *Basic* Technology Adoption

Together these countries account for 11% of total East Asian GDP. These countries are not at the same level of development, nor do they share much commonality in business practices, customs, or languages.

Development and technology acceptance are ranked in the order of the bullets listed immediately above, with Singapore being just behind Japan as the most technologically advanced country in Asia. Many Western companies locate their headquarters for the southern part of Asia in Singapore because of its business-friendly laws, IP protection, English-speaking citizens, and low taxes.

3. Greater China

- **Mainland China** – *Mid-Level* Technology Adoption
- **Hong Kong and Taiwan** – *Advanced* Technology Adoption

Taiwan and Hong Kong – These are advanced economies with a high level of technology acceptance, Internet use, and a wide variety of business sizes, which translate into strong markets for enterprise software. Taiwan has a large electronics manufacturing industry and is one of the world's leaders in manufacturing computer components. Hong Kong is neck and neck with Singapore as the southern part of Asia's largest financial center, is a world financial center, and has been China's banker for dealing with the outside world. Despite these advantages, both are small markets with a combined population of approximately thirty million—one-half the size of one of the large European countries such as France or the UK. However, as was stated above, both of these territories face uncertain futures because of an empowered China looming over them:

- **Taiwan** – Considered a wayward territory by China and under the threat of being taken over by force

- **Hong Kong** – The threat that China will lessen its autonomy and eliminate its unique economic freedoms

Mainland China – Its economy continues to grow at an annual rate of almost 10%, as it has for the last 30 years. A major growth driver has been the build-out of its manufacturing capability, transportation infrastructure, and an ever-increasing number of buildings of all kinds: office, industrial, and housing units for the millions from the country-side who are swarming to its major cities. As construction and exports of manufactured goods rise, the major opportunities for growth of technology and sophisticated enterprise software are limited. Instead, the trend is to exploit China's advantage of cheap and plentiful labor.

There are more than 700 million cellphone users in China, more than twice the U.S. population, but only 10% of cell phones used in China have 3G connectivity[xxvi] with the capability of running mobile Internet and Apps. However, since the population is so huge, even if only a small percentage can afford smartphones and PCs, it is still a large user base. As an example, Apple stores in China gross more per square foot than any other Apple stores in the world. That is astounding considering Apple prices its goods at Western price levels in China, even though the Chinese median family income is approximately one-eighth that of the U.S. in 2010 currency exchange rates.[xxvii]

The rapid-growth environment in China has not resulted in as large an enterprise software market as its economic strength might suggest. Its 2010 GDP is 13.6% of the world's total, while its software market is just 5.1% of the world's total. This disparity could be due partly to China's high software piracy rate of 70%. The vast majority of Chinese medium and enterprise businesses are low-tech, with dependence on abundant cheap labor rather than using technology to increase productivity. Despite the dated perception that a high percentage of Chinese GDP is generated by inefficient state-run enterprises, *The Economist*[xxviii] recently estimated that 70% of GDP is now produced by private enterprise, which equates to a high percentage of the forty-three million businesses in China. However, many of the emerging private businesses in China operate quasi-legally. Local representatives of the central government bureaucracy apparently do not want to know if businesses are following government regulations, which are selectively enforced. According to the same article from *The Economist* referenced just above, "Chinese regulation of its private sector is often referred to 'one eye open, one eye shut.'" With this kind of uncertainty and lack of availability of long-term capital, it is too risky for Chinese businesses to invest in technology or, more specifically, large enterprise software.

4. India – *Basic* to *Mid-Level* Technology Adoption

With its rapid population growth, it is estimated that India will supplant China as the world's most populous nation around 2050. However, India is still a developing country with GDP PPP per person at US $3,300, approximately 30% of the world's average GDP per person. Much of India's basic infrastructure (roads, airports, telecommunications, and wireless communications) are nearing a breaking point, as the Indian economy continues its growth at 8–10% per year for the foreseeable future. The local Indian enterprise software market is underdeveloped, despite several large and well-known export-oriented outsourced IT businesses and the presence of local operations of large tech companies (IBM, Microsoft, Accenture), which are focused on both development and outsourced services. India's biggest resource is the large number of well-educated, English-speaking locals who can be hired at low salaries in terms of current exchange rates.

The Indian market pricing level for technology products is extremely low, on the order of 10%–20% of the price level of developed countries. The local market has high protectionist trade barriers, which are disappearing slowly. There are millions of sole-proprietors and micro-businesses catering to the massive but poor Indian domestic market. Of the tens of millions of businesses in India, relatively few are medium and enterprise businesses and many of these are labor-intensive and not technologically advanced. At this point in time, India is a challenging market for most enterprise software vendors to enter for a questionable rate of return.

Looking next at quantitative measures for technology acceptance, **Figure 26** summarizes wealth and shows total software market sizes and Internet usage as a percent of the total population for the East Asian economies. The U.S. and Australia are added for reference.

Country	GDP per Person / Total GDP	# People (million)	Total Software Market		Internet Users		
			2010 Total / Tech Adoption	2010-13 Forecasted Growth	Actual (million)	World Rank	% of People
U.S.	$46,900 $14,630 billion	312	$130.0 bill. advanced	5.4%	240	2	77%
Australia	$39,000 $ 880 billion	23	$ 4.0 billion advanced	7.0%	17	27	80%
China	$7,500 $10,100 bill.	1,343	$16.7 billion mid-level	12.3%	420	1	31%
Taiwan	$35,500 $ 820 billion	23	$1.4 billion advanced	8.9%	16	29	69%
Hong Kong	$45,400	7	$0.5 billion advanced	7.6%	5	49	70%
Greater China	$7,900 $10,900 billion	1,373	$18.6 billion	12.0%	441		32%
Japan	$33,800 $ 4,300 billion	127	$14.2 billion advanced	4.1%	99	4	78%
South Korea	$30,000 $ 1,460 billion	49	$2.7 billion advanced	7.9%	39	11	80%
Japan + Korea	$ 32,800 $5,770 billion	176	$16.9 billion	4.7%	138		78%
Singapore	$57,100 $ 290 billion	5	$ 1.1 billion advanced	7.7%	4	63	78%
Indonesia	$4,300 $ 1,030 billion	238	$ 1.1 billion advanced	11.8%	30	16	13%

Country	GDP per Person / Total GDP	# People (million)	Total Software Market		Internet Users		
			2010 Total / Tech Adoption	2010-13 Forecasted Growth	Actual (million)	World Rank	% of People
Malay-sia	$14,900 $ 410 billion	28	$ 0.7 billion mid-level	8.4%	17	28	62%
TOTAL: 3 Above	$6,400 $ 1,730 billion	270	$ 2.9 billion	9.4%	51		19%
India	$ 3,400 $ 4,000 billion	1,194	$2.0 billion basic	11.5%	81	3	7%
TOTAL: Top 9, EAST ASIA	$7,400 $22,400 billion	3,013	$40.4 billion	9.0%	711		24%

Figure 26 – EAST ASIA: GDP, Population, Total Software Markets[x,] Internet Usage[xi]

The 2010–2013 forecasted software market growth rate for East Asia is lower than Europe's forecast: 9.0% for the East Asian countries vs. 10.2% for Europe. Japan, which is approximately one-third of the total East Asian software market, drags down the overall growth rate with its anemic growth, forecasted to be 4.1% annually from 2010-2013.

There are large contrasts between the Asian regions in Internet usage rates, which highlight the vast differences in technology acceptance. The advanced countries including Japan, South Korea, Taiwan, Singapore, and Hong Kong have Internet usage rates in the high 70% range, similar to the U.S. and European countries. The less developed countries have significantly lower Internet usage rates: Mainland China at 32%, Indonesia at 12% and India with only 7% of its population using the Internet.

Figure 27 summarizes 2010 software markets, 2010-2013 growth rates, percentage of regional and world totals, and 2013 forecasted total software market sizes for East Asia. Again, the U.S. and Australia are added for reference:

| Country | 2010 Total Software Market ($ billions) | Software Market % of Total | | 2010 – 2013 Forecasted Growth | 2013 Forecast | |
		% East Asia Top 9	% World		Total Software Market ($ billions)	% World
U.S.	$130.0	308.1%	40.0%	5.4%	$152.0	37.2%
China	$16.7	39.0%	5.1%	12.3%	$23.7	5.8%
Taiwan	$ 1.4	3.3%	0.4%	8.9%	$ 1.8	0.4%
Hong Kong	$ 0.5	1.2%	0.2%	7.6%	$ 0.6	0.2%
Greater China	$18.6	43.5%	5.7%	12.0%	$26.1	6.4%
Japan	$14.2	33.2%	4.4%	4.1%	$16.0	3.9%
South Korea	$ 2.7	6.2%	0.8%	7.9%	$ 3.3	0.8%
Japan + Korea	$16.9	39.4%	5.2%	4.7%	$19.3	4.7%
India	$ 2.0	4.8%	0.6%	11.5%	$ 2.8	0.7%
Singapore	$ 1.1	2.6%	0.3%	7.7%	$ 1.4	0.3%
Indonesia	$ 1.1	2.5%	0.3%	11.8%	$ 1.5	0.4%
Malaysia	$ 0.7	1.6%	0.2%	8.4%	$ 0.9	0.2%
TOTAL: 3 Above	$ 2.9	6.7%	0.9%	9.4%	$ 3.8	0.9%
TOTAL: Top 9, East Asia	$ 42.2	98.5%	13.0%	9.0%	$ 54.6	13.3%

Figure 27 – EAST ASIA: 2010-2013 Total Software Market Sizes, Growth Rates, % of Total Region & World

Most of the software markets in East Asia are forecasted to grow faster from 2010–2013 than the world baseline rate of 8% per year. The notable exception is Japan, which is forecasted to grow at only 4.1% annually over the same period. From 2010-2013 East Asia's percentage of worldwide software is forecasted to barely budge from 13% in 2010 to 13.3% in 2013. This is attributable to slow-growth Japan, which accounts for one-third of the total East Asian software market.

Figure 28 illustrates the East Asian software markets graphically, comparing the total software market sizes by country to GDP PPP by country for the East Asian markets:

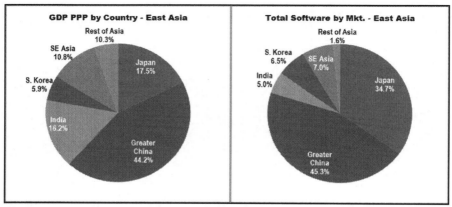

Figure 28 – EAST ASIA: GDP vs. Total Software Market Sizes

Figure 29 ranks the East Asian countries/regions from top to bottom for highest shares of the combined East Asian software markets as compared to their share of total East Asian GDP:

| Country | % of Total East Asia | | | Software Sales as % of GDP |
	Software Market Size	GDP PPP	Index (see footnote xxix)	
Japan	34.7%	17.5%	198	0.26%
South Korea	6.5%	5.9%	110	0.26%
Greater China	45.3%	44.2%	102	0.32%
Singapore	7.0%	10.8%	65	0.57%
Malaysia				0.32%
Indonesia				0.16%
India	5.0%	16.2%	31	0.14%
TOTAL: East Asia			100	0.28%

Figure 29 – Top East Asian Comparison of GDP Share to Total Software Market Share

Not surprisingly, the contrasts between the East Asian countries are significant in the comparisons between shares of GDP and total software market sizes:

- Japan has almost twice the share of the total East Asia total software market as its GDP: 35% share of software vs. 17.5% of GDP;
- South Korea and Greater China's shares of East Asia's total software markets and total GDP are roughly equal;
- Singapore, Malaysia, and Indonesia's total software shares are roughly two-thirds of their GDP shares;
- India's total software market share is one-third of its GDP share.

Another approach to assessing technology acceptance across countries is the World Economic Forum's network readiness index (NRI), which was described directly before **Figure 7** on page 20 and a custom index to measure "readiness to embrace to enterprise software" on the same scale: 1 (low) to 7 (high). **Figure 30** illustrates the NRI and custom index results for East Asia and other selected countries:

	NRI Index					Custom Index: Enterprise Software (Scale of 1 to 7, low to high)							
						12.5%	22.5%	12.5%	15.0%	12.5%	25.0%	100%	
	Index Score (1-7, LO-HI)	World Rank: '10-'11	Change: '10→'11	World Rank: '06-'07	Change: '07→'11	Avail. Of Latest Tech.	Laws Relating to ICT	Avail. - Scientists & Eng.	Buyer Sophistication	Extent of Staff Training	Co. Level of Tech. Absorp.	CUSTOM INDEX	CUSTOM INDEX, Sing. = 100
East Asia													
Singapore	5.59	2	0	3	1	6.3	5.9	5.3	4.6	5.5	6.0	5.66	100
Japan	4.95	19	2	14	-5	6.3	4.7	5.8	5.2	5.4	6.3	5.60	99
Taiwan	5.30	6	5	13	7	5.8	5.3	6.5	4.7	4.7	6.1	5.42	96
South Korea	5.19	10	5	19	9	6.1	5.1	4.9	4.6	4.4	6.1	5.29	94
Hong Kong	5.19	12	-4	12	0	6.4	5.5	4.1	4.4	4.7	5.9	5.27	93
Malaysia	4.74	28	-1	26	-2	5.7	5.1	4.7	4.1	5.0	5.5	5.06	90
India	4.03	48	-5	44	-4	5.6	4.5	5.2	3.8	4.1	5.3	4.77	84
China	4.35	36	1	59	23	4.4	4.4	4.6	4.6	4.1	4.9	4.54	80
Indonesia	3.92	53	14	62	9	4.8	3.9	4.7	3.9	4.4	4.9	4.43	78
Selected Other Countries													
U.S.	5.33	5	0	7	2	6.4	5.4	5.7	4.5	5.1	6.0	5.54	98
Canada	5.21	8	-1	11	3	6.4	5.5	5.6	4.7	5.0	5.6	5.47	97
Australia	5.06	17	-1	15	-2	6.1	5.5	4.5	4.4	4.8	5.9	5.30	94
New Zealand	5.03	18	1	22	4	6.0	5.5	4.1	4.0	4.8	5.9	5.18	92
Sweden	5.60	1	0	2	1	6.8	5.9	5.8	5.0	5.7	6.4	5.97	105
Norway	5.21	9	1	10	1	6.7	5.6	5.1	4.5	5.5	6.2	5.65	100
U.K.	5.12	15	-2	9	-6	6.4	5.4	4.8	4.6	4.7	5.7	5.32	94
France	4.92	20	-2	23	3	6.4	5.2	5.3	4.1	4.7	5.6	5.24	93
Germany	5.14	13	1	16	3	6.3	5.3	4.8	4.4	5.2	6.0	5.39	95
Israel	4.81	22	6	18	-4	6.4	4.5	5.1	3.4	4.7	6.1	5.07	90
Brazil	3.90	56	5	53	-3	5.5	4.5	4.0	3.6	4.2	5.2	4.57	81

Figure 30 – EAST ASIA: NRI and Custom Enterprise Software Readiness Index

As might be expected, the East Asian countries discussed above as the best for technology acceptance have the top rankings in the "readiness to embrace enterprise software" custom index: Taiwan and Hong Kong from Greater China, Japan and South Korea from northeast Asia, and Singapore and Malaysia from southeast Asia.

Best for Wealth and Technology Acceptance

There is not much commonality across the countries of East Asia. Assessing both *Wealth* and *Technology Acceptance*, the following are the best markets for enterprise software vendors to begin selling in East Asia. To repeat, the order for market entry in East Asia is hard to generalize.

1. The Developed Countries of Japan and South Korea

Together these countries make up almost 25% of total East Asian GDP and are in the *Wealthy* range of GDP per person: US $33,800 and US $30,000 respectively. Their software markets combined make up 41% of the East Asian total.

Technology acceptance in both countries is high with Japan as the most technologically advanced country in East Asia. There are many medium and enterprise businesses in both countries, including world-class consumer electronics, manufacturing, and financial services companies that export around the world: Samsung, Hyundai, LG, Sony, Toyota, Fujitsu, and Nintendo, to name a few. The presence of these worldwide giants means there are numerous smaller businesses in both Japan and South Korea that support the local operations of these well-known enterprises. That creates a fertile market for enterprise software.

Evidence of Japan's high technology acceptance is its total software market of US $14.2 billion, sixth largest in the world behind the U.S., Germany, the UK, France, and China. Japan also scores second to Singapore in East Asia in its "readiness to embrace enterprise software" index at 5.60 on a scale of 1 – 7, sixth in the world. South Korea is not far behind on this index at 5.29, fourth in East Asia.

2. Three of the Five Countries that make up Southeast Asia: Singapore, Malaysia, Indonesia

Together these three countries account for almost 11% of East Asian GDP, with the following GDPs per person (currencies are US $):

a. Singapore, the third highest GDP PPP per person in the world, is $57,000

b. *Middle Income* Malaysia has GDP PPP per person of $15,000

c. *Developing* Indonesia has GDP PPP per person of $4,300. Indonesia is the fourth most populous country in the world and has high potential, because its business environment is rapidly improving

The combined software markets for these three countries account for only 7% of total East Asian software. Although diverse in stage of development and cultures, these three are close geographically.

Technology acceptance in Singapore rivals Japan and a significant number of Western multinationals have located their Asian headquarters in Singapore, which in turn has increased technology acceptance. Singapore scores the highest in East Asia for its "readiness to embrace enterprise software" index at 5.66, as well as being the third highest in the world behind Sweden and Switzerland. Malaysia and Indonesia both have lower technology acceptance. However, they are modernizing their economies, growing rapidly, and establishing a base of medium and large organizations that are considering technology investments, including enterprise software.

Greater China (Mainland China, Hong Kong, and Taiwan) has tremendous potential and has grown to become a major part of the worldwide GDP PPP (15%), East Asian GDP PPP (44%) and its software market as a percentage of the total East Asian software (45%). Even so, the territories comprising Greater China are not where enterprise software vendors typically initiate their sales expansion into East Asia. This is due to the challenging business climate and relatively low technology acceptance throughout Mainland China, which accounts for 90% of Greater China GDP. China has a relatively low score of 4.54 in the custom "readiness to embrace enterprise software" index compared to the more advanced East Asian countries at 5.27 and above. Mainland China also has the significant disadvantage of weak IP protection, and many local Chinese companies are hungry to take advantage of this, implementing business practices that would be considered immoral or illegal in the U.S. and Europe. Despite the uncertain futures of Hong Kong and Taiwan, their technology acceptance is high with custom software indices of 5.27 and 5.42, respectively, just behind Singapore.

East Asia: Acceptance of English as a Language for Commerce

As was described in the previous sections, English as a language for commerce is crucial when considering market entry for enterprise software sales, because it is the most widely spoken language in technology. Assuming that most enterprise software is initially written in English, many vendors start international expansion in English-speaking countries and places where English is widely used and understood in the business world. This enables the cost for translating the software into other languages to be deferred and allows software vendors to gain international field experience to better understand the required order of other languages.

Examining the East Asian countries that are at the top for *Wealth* and *Acceptance of Technology*—and adding in India and China—here are the primary languages of business commerce in East Asia. The list is sorted from most to least English friendly:

- **Singapore**

  English has been the official language of business and government ever since Singapore broke away from Malaysia to become a separate country 50 years ago, two years after both Singapore and Malaysia gained independence from the UK. Since that time, schools have been teaching exclusively in English. This has resulted in universal English fluency for those under the age of 50. Depending on the Singaporean's heritage (Chinese, Indian, or Malay), children generally learn their native language at home and learn English once they start school. Those of Chinese heritage tend to learn both their native Chinese dialect and Mandarin at home.

  Enterprise software products, web sites, and marketing materials in English are adequate in Singapore. When products and sales materials are translated into Chinese for the Greater China markets, Singaporean buyers of Chinese descent will benefit from this as well.

- **India**

  India gained independence from the UK in 1947. English is taught in schools, but not exclusively, as it is in Singapore. There are hundreds of languages spoken in India. Hindu and English are the most widely spoken, especially among business professionals and government officials. Despite widely distributed jokes in the U.S. about the Indian accents of call center personnel, highlighted in the popular sitcom *Outsourced*, most Indian professionals know the language well enough to use English enterprise software with ease.

Enterprise software products, web sites, and marketing materials in English are acceptable in India.

- **Malaysia**

Although English is widely spoken among Chinese and Indian professionals in Malaysia because of its heritage as an English colony; the country's primary language is Malay. Among the Malays, the native race in Malaysia who number approximately 50% of the population, English is less widely spoken. Many of the Chinese and Indians, who make up 30% of the population, speak English.

Until recently, businesses were required to employ a quota of Malays and be majority-owned by a Malaysian, blunting the business prowess of the entrepreneurial Chinese in this country. These laws are slowly being eliminated as Malaysia modernizes its economy.

English enterprise software products, web sites, and marketing materials function well in Malaysia, especially among the professional Indians and Chinese. As in Singapore, when products and sales materials are translated into Chinese for the Greater China markets, Malaysian buyers of Chinese descent will benefit from this. At this point, translation of software, web sites, and marketing materials into Malay is probably not worth the incremental revenue that would be gained from Malaysia.

- **Indonesia**

This country's primary language is Indonesian. It is spoken by all and most people also speak a second regional language learned at home. Children are educated in Indonesian. There is some English spoken in business, but appreciably less than in Singapore, India, and Malaysia. Younger people tend to speak more English because of their exposure to the Internet, social media, videos and English-language television and movies.

Only a specialized product, such as data center software or enterprise resource planning (ERP) software for large organizations, will work in English. Any other enterprise software product will have to be translated into Indonesian, which is a double-byte language. Web sites and marketing material will also need to be translated into Indonesian. At this point, translation of software, web sites and marketing materials into

Indonesian is probably not worth the incremental revenue that would be gained from Indonesia.

- **South Korea**

  Except for young people and workers in tourism, little English is spoken in South Korea. More English tends to be spoken within the large multinationals such as Samsung and Hyundai, though it is unknown exactly what percentage speak English in these large enterprises. Similar to Indonesia, younger people in South Korea tend to speak more English because of their exposure to the Internet, social media, videos and English-language television and movies.

  To sell an enterprise software product requires translation of the software into Korean, a double-byte language. Web sites and marketing materials will need to be translated into Korean as well.

- **Japan**

  Only a very few speak English in Japan. This might be related to Japan's inward-looking culture, which emerged when the country closed itself to the outside world for 700 years. As a result, the Japanese thrive on living and doing business in isolation, in their native language.

  To sell an enterprise software product requires translation of the software into Japanese, a double-byte language. Web sites and marketing materials will need to be translated into Japanese as well.

- **Greater China**

  Although the country has many hundreds of dialects and languages, the central government has worked diligently to standardize Mandarin as the language of government and business. This language has the greatest number of native speakers in the world. Similar to Indonesia, many Chinese children learn to speak a regional or local language at home and then learn Mandarin in school. English is not widely used in most parts of Mainland China. The highest number of English speakers can be found in the in the metropolises of Shanghai and Beijing, generally more than Japan, but still not significant in number. Taiwan has similar speaking patterns to the mainland.

  In Hong Kong, Cantonese is the most common language. Although many Hong Kong natives can speak Mandarin, they prefer to use Cantonese. But there has been an influx of Mandarin speakers from Mainland China since Hong Kong's takeover in 1997. English was formerly an official language in Hong Kong, and it is spoken by 3% of the population daily and by another additional 35% as a second language.[xxx] Some limited types of enterprise software might be salable in English, but in general, an enterprise software product in Hong Kong requires translation into Mandarin Chinese, a double-byte language.

Across Greater China, to sell an enterprise software product requires translation of the software into Mandarin, a double-byte language. Web sites and marketing materials will also require translation into Mandarin Chinese.

As a side note, it is more complicated to translate software into Asian languages, most of which require double-byte character support (DBCS). A double-byte language has more than 256 characters to represent, which means two bytes of storage are required for each character. For recent software code written with modern tools such as Microsoft's .NET, DBCS is not much of an issue other than translation and reconstruction of user interfaces. For older code, adding DBCS support in order that the software can be translated into a double-byte language is a major programming effort, sometimes requiring a total rewrite.

East Asia: The Technology Sales and Buying Culture

As described above, this measurement is based on the similarity of the market's technology evaluation and buying practices to those of the U.S. and the large economies of Western Europe. These territories are chosen as benchmarks because they are the dominant enterprise software markets. Additionally, part of assessing the technology sales and buying culture is the all-important availability of qualified people for staffing international sales operation start-up. The most important functions for starting out are:

1. **Sales Staff** – Those who can sell directly as well as through channels.

2. **Technical Staff** – Those having strong people skills for presales support, for training channel partners, and having the technical knowledge to drive consultative sales.

Singapore is the only country in East Asia that has a sales and buying culture for enterprise software that is reasonably similar to the U.S. and Western Europe. The countries after Singapore are presented in this section in no particular order.

1. Singapore – *Advanced* Technology Adoption

In East Asia, Singapore has the most similar buying culture to the U.S. and Western Europe. As was described in the sections above, English is the official business language and there are many Western multinationals that have domiciled their South Asian headquarters in Singapore. Their presence drives the sale of sophisticated enterprise software, as do other Singaporean companies that support these large enterprises.

Singapore is considered to be of the world's financial centers and is ranked fourth on the 2010 Global Financial Centres index,[xxxi] as well as fourth on the Worldwide Centres of Commerce Index. Singapore's port is one of the busiest in the world as measured by shipping tonnage. It is the world's busiest container port, as well as the world's busiest transshipment port.[xxxii] Additionally, Singapore is the major point of entry for Middle Eastern oil destined for East Asia. Consequently, the Singaporean enterprise software market is much larger than expected for a country of its size, and sales of software to headquarters in Singapore can lead to additional sales to other Asian operations within the same organization.

The sales process in Singapore is similar to the U.S. and Western Europe, though there might be slightly more emphasis on price negotiation. Some software vendors increase the list price for Singapore and other Asian markets to have the leeway to grant a larger discount. There is little visible corruption in Singapore because the penalties are so harsh. As a result, Singapore is one of the least corrupt countries in the world.

Technical staff for supporting enterprise software sales is relatively plentiful in Singapore, but unemployment hovers around 2%. The demand for local techs is high, thus increasing the costs of employing them. Talented sales staff is hard to find, as it seems Singaporeans identify with formulaic approaches, which doesn't correspond with the complex solution selling required for enterprise software. Many enterprise software vendors selling in Singapore hire expatriates rather than employing local Singaporeans.

The following chart, **Figure 31,** illustrates the breakdown of total technology spending by vertical segment for Singapore, with comparison to the countries nearby geographically: Indonesia, Malaysia, as well as Total East Asia:

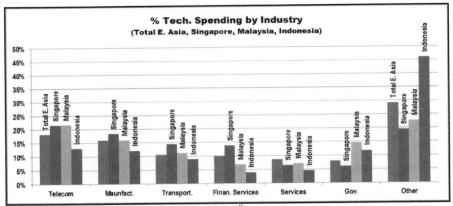

Figure 31 – Total Technology Spending[xxii] by Leading Industry Segments: Singapore, Malaysia, Indonesia

Despite its significant differences from other East Asian countries in size, demographics, wealth, and singular focus on attracting East Asian headquarters operations, Singapore's mix of industry segments doesn't vary that much from total East Asia other than the financial services segment. Financial Services accounts for 14% of its technology spending compared to 10% of total East Asia and much less for Malaysia and Indonesia, where financial services account for 5% of total technology spending.

After Singapore, the sales and buying cultures in East Asia diverge widely from the U.S. and Europe. The following are listed in no particular order.

2. Other Small Countries of Southeast Asia:
- **Malaysia, Thailand –** *Mid-Level* Technology Adoption
- **Indonesia –** *Basic* Technology Adoption

These three countries have little commonality in terms of sales and buying cultures, business practices, or language. Nevertheless, they are close enough geographically to locate a regional sales office in Singapore for selling across the entire region.

Malaysia – After Singapore, Malaysia is the most developed country of this group. Here, the buying practices for enterprise software are changing, as the country evolves from Malay staffing quotas and majority ownership. In the traditional Malaysian way of doing business, payoffs to Malays were common. However, as the laws change and business procedures are modernized, Malaysia's buying practices will move closer to the U.S. and European way of evaluating software on its business and technical merits. But Malaysia is not there yet. For anything but the largest enterprise software products in the data center, selling in Malaysia, direct or through channel partners, requires staff who can speak Malay and know how to shepherd a sale through to completion.

Although technical staff to support enterprise software sales in Malaysia is harder to find than in Singapore, lower-level staff is available, especially those of Chinese and Indian ancestry. Finding native Malay techs is more difficult, but they are very valuable because of their native language skills and insight into the Malaysian business culture. Talented sales staff is hard to find in Malaysia. Consequently, many enterprise software vendors resort to hiring expatriates to sell rather than locals. However, the lack of Malay speaking skills is a hindrance.

Indonesia – This country has made great strides in modernizing its economy since its dictator, Suharto, was deposed fifteen years ago. During Suharto's tenure, nothing could be sold without someone close to the dictator or his family receiving a payoff. This is not the case anymore and the transition to buying enterprise software on its merits is improving, but remains a long way off. Selling in Indonesia, direct or through channel partners, requires staff who can speak Indonesian and know how to close a business transaction without violating the U.S. Foreign Corrupt Practices Act.

Hiring technical staff with enterprise software skills to support sales in Indonesia is challenging. Many Indonesians with IT training and skills have left for Singapore or Malaysia in search of better employment prospects. There hasn't been quite enough development in Indonesia for these technology-experienced natives to return home, unlike the trend of Chinese in the U.S returning to China to seek opportunity in their homeland.

Thailand – Until the early 2000s, Thailand was one the best markets for enterprise software in the southern part of Asia. However, since then there have been many government changes and some military intervention, which has disrupted business. This has slowed economic growth and destroyed business confidence to the point where Thailand is not a good market to enter for enterprise software sales

Figure 31, on page 72 compares the breakdown of total technology spending by industry by vertical segment for Singapore, Malaysia, and Indonesia to total East Asia. Malaysia's market segments outside the East Asian norm are less spending on telecom and more on its government segment. Indonesia also has several outlier segments for spending percentages: lower than other East Asian countries in telecom and financial services and higher in others such as wholesale distribution and natural resources.

3. Japan and South Korea – *Advanced* Technology Adoption

Geographically close to each other on the northeast corner of Asia, both of these economies are advanced with a broad range of target medium and large organizations in the market for sophisticated enterprise software. Both have characteristics and buying patterns similar to each other but dissimilar from the rest of the world.

The Japanese and South Koreans don't get along well because of a long history of conquests and occupations between them. It is difficult for a single sales office to cover both territories, as few natives in either country speak both Korean and Japanese, and they have a mutual suspicion of each other. Especially sensitive are older South Koreans, who remember Japan's brutal occupation of Korea from 1910–1945.

Japan – This country is extreme by virtue of its unique culture, inward focus, and many other characteristics, including how businesses and distribution channels operate. These factors affect how enterprise software vendors sell in Japan, as well as creating and operating channels there. Establishing relationships with Japanese enterprise software channel partners is crucial for entering the Japanese market. For example, large enterprise companies in Japan, such as the national telecom company (NTT), multinational manufacturers, and the largest banks and insurance companies, prefer to buy enterprise software from their chosen Japanese resellers/integrators (collectively called "channel partners") rather than directly from the software vendor. Many Japanese channel partners have translated software and performed systems integration on behalf their clients for many years, which has resulted in a deep knowledge of their clients' systems:

- Know their clients' IT environments and business requirements well

- Understand their clients' Japanese language and business process requirements

Software vendors who seek to establish a presence in the large Japanese enterprise market have little choice but to sell through the preferred channel partners of large enterprises rather than selling direct. This decreases profit margin for most Japanese sales operations, as Japanese channel partners are customarily paid a larger commission than channel partners elsewhere, generally ten to fifteen percentage points higher per sale. Even when an enterprise software vendor has established direct sales in Japan, a significant portion of sales destined for large enterprises will be through these preferred channel partners.

Large enterprises are an important component of the target market for enterprise software in Japan. But there is also a significant number of medium to large businesses that have a high proclivity to streamline and automate their business processes using enterprise software. Selling to them requires native Japanese salespeople because of the language barrier and their understanding the decision-making process in Japanese organizations. To summarize: the process of reaching a business decision in Japan is called "ringi," and for any non-trivial decision such as buying enterprise software, a team of people is usually charged to make the decision. Unanimous consent is required and it is impossible to predict when a decision will be reached. This makes it extremely difficult for an enterprise software vendor to forecast when a Japanese deal will close.

As for finding sales and technical staff in Japan, talent is very expensive and English speakers are paid an additional premium. In a business and decision-making environment such as this, local enterprise software sales managers who can translate Japanese sales situations/status into the rough U.S. equivalent are indispensible and hard to find.

South Korea – The sales and decision-making process in South Korea is similar in many ways to Japan but not as extreme. Incidentally, this is not something to point out to South Koreans or Japanese because of the sensitivities between the countries, as mentioned above. Note that despite its rapid growth and modernization, South Korea is still approximately one-third the size of Japan in population and GDP PPP, and has fewer medium and enterprise organizations as targets for enterprise software.

Although this is a subjective perspective derived from years of selling enterprise software into Japan and South Korea, South Koreans seem to want to change their business practices to align more closely with the U.S. and Europe, whereas the Japanese seem proud of their differences and want to maintain their separate identity.

Similar to the Japanese enterprise companies, the business conglomerates in South Korea (chaebols) also have opaque decision-making processes. However, once a decision is made to purchase a capital asset such as enterprise software, sales to other members of a chaebol are streamlined with a reference from another member company.

Figure 32 compares the breakdown of total technology spending by vertical segment for Japan, South Korea, and the two other advanced countries/special regions of Singapore and Hong Kong, as well as total East Asia:

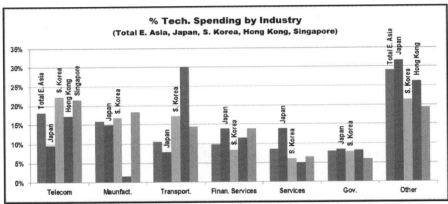

Figure 32 – Total Technology Spending[xxii] by Leading Industry Segments: Japan, S. Korea, Hong Kong, Singapore

Other than the manufacturing and government segments, technology spending by segment in Japan and South Korea differs significantly from each other and from the spending by segment of total East Asia.

4. Greater China

- **Mainland China –** *Mid-Level* **Technology Adoption**
- **Hong Kong and Taiwan –** *Advanced* **Technology Adoption**

China – Despite the entrepreneurial business culture developed over several thousand years and expatriate Chinese influence all over the southern part of Asia from the exodus of 1949, Chinese businesses exhibit a different morality than Western business practices in areas such as patents, IP protection, industrial espionage, and thievery. A patchwork of complicated local and national laws and regulations are selectively enforced and favor local companies. Despite the promise of China's huge market potential, initiating sales and doing business is fraught with difficulty and saddled with high rates of failure for many reasons:

- opaque local business practices
- difficulty enforcing contracts
- lack of IP and patent protection
- favoritism for local companies in regulation and law enforcement
- the language barrier
- low prices in the local market

Mainland China is not usually the first location of choice for enterprise software vendors to initiate their sales expansion into East Asia.

Hong Kong and Taiwan – These areas look promising on the surface, but their future is uncertain based on Chinese favoring Shanghai and Beijing over Hong Kong and Taiwan's uneasy relations with its huge and increasingly strident neighbor. However, both have larger markets for enterprise software than their size might indicate because of:

- **Hong Kong** – A large presence of multinational financial services, foreign exchange, and trading operations
- **Taiwan** – A large PC and component manufacturing industry

Other than the Chinese language barrier, selling into these strong industry segments is similar to selling to other multinationals around the world.

Mandarin language skills are absolutely required when an enterprise software vendor begins selling into Mainland China, Taiwan, or Hong Kong. Cantonese language skills are highly desirable in Hong Kong despite the fact that almost 40% of people in Hong Kong speak some English.

On the Chinese mainland, understanding how to overcome local software competition and protecting software IP from local Chinese companies is hard for an outsider to comprehend. Additionally, negotiating a deal, getting a customer contract signed, and negotiating a channel partner or joint venture deal requires local legal expertise and staff experienced in doing business in China. Finally, an experienced law firm from outside China is required to help set up the Chinese subsidiary correctly. If this is not done properly, a Chinese operation could be invalidated and the parent software vendor could be fined or barred from operating in China.

The following chart, **Figure 33**, compares the breakdown of total technology spending by industry for China, Hong Kong and Taiwan, with India, and Total East Asia added for comparison:

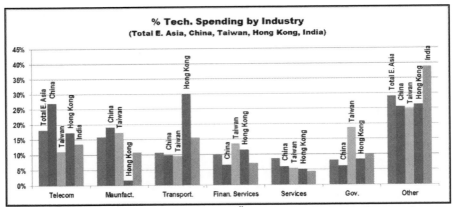

Figure 33 – Total Technology Spending[xxii] by Leading Industry Segments: China, Taiwan, Hong Kong, India

The country segments for total technology spending that stand out for their differences are:

1. **China, Telecom** spending – at 27% of total technology spending, which is much higher than total East Asia and Hong Kong at 18% and 17% respectively. India and Taiwan are both much lower in the 10% – 15% range.

2. **Hong Kong, Manufacturing** spending – at less than 2%, very much lower than anywhere else in Asia. This is because Hong Kong is one of the major financial capitals in China and manufacturing is done elsewhere in China, where costs are much lower and space for large manufacturing facilities is more plentiful.

3. **Hong Kong, Transportation** spending – at 30% of total technology spending, double the rate of anywhere else in Asia. One would expect the other major transportation hub in the southern part of East Asia, Singapore, to be equally as high. Surprisingly, Singapore's technology spending on the Transportation sector is only 14% of its total.

4. **Taiwan, Government** spending – much higher than anywhere else in East Asia at 19% of total technology spending. No other country is above 10%.

In terms of absolute numbers, Mainland China technology spending dominates Greater China with 90% of the total. In other words, total technology spending in Taiwan and Hong Kong combined is one-ninth the spending China mainland.

5. India – *Basic* Technology Adoption

With its rapid population growth, India is forecasted to supplant China as the world's most populous nation over the next thirty to forty years. However, of the approximately fifty million businesses in India, two-thirds are sole proprietors, and fewer than one million businesses have ten or more employees[xxxiii]. Outside of the Western companies that have outsourced call centers, local programming, and other business processes, as well as the Indian companies that provide these services, medium and enterprise companies in India tend to be inefficient and exploit their competitive advantage of cheap labor rather than increasing productivity and automating processes using sophisticated enterprise software.

There are many tariffs and legislative barriers to overcome when exporting to India. This has improved over time as the Indian market opens up, but government bureaucracy and endless regulations are still challenges for foreign companies setting up Indian subsidiaries.

Another challenge that is difficult for enterprise software vendors to overcome is the low price level. In India, enterprise software vendors can only set prices at 10% – 20% of the U.S. and Western Europe levels. Although local English-speaking technical labor is in good supply at a fraction of the cost of employing a technician in the U.S. or Europe, it is difficult to generate reasonable margins at such a low price levels.

India is usually not high on the priority list for East Asia market entry for most enterprise software vendors because of the challenges outlined above.

To investigate the best industry segments for enterprise software vendors to target in India, **Figure 34** illustrates the breakdown of total technology spending by industry segment, with comparison to the countries close to India's GDP per person, Indonesia and China, along with total East Asia:

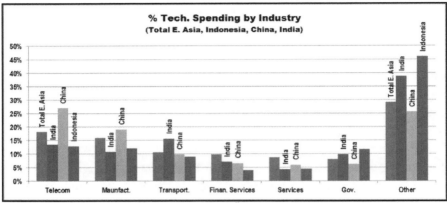

Figure 34 – Total Technology Spending[xxii] by Leading Industry Segments: India, China, Indonesia

The only segment in India that differs much from Total East Asia, China, and Indonesia is in Transportation, with India at 16% and the others clustered around 10% of total technology spending.

Putting It All Together: East Asia Sales and Buying Cultures

In summary, the technology sales and buying cultures across East Asia vary dramatically, with Singapore the only country with a culture somewhat similar to the U.S. and Western Europe. The best way to consider expansion into these territories is to weigh the pros and cons of each of the four major areas:

1. Southeast Asia – Singapore, Malaysia, Indonesia
2. Japan and Korea
3. Greater China – Mainland China, Hong Kong, and Taiwan
4. India

There is no set order for market entry in East Asia, as each of these areas has its own distinct sales and buying cultures and unique challenges for U.S. or European enterprise software vendors. Entering the East Asian markets requires cultural flexibility and hiring experienced people who know how to sell, manage channels and support sales across these distinct business cultures and vast geographies.

East Asia: Summary – Results from 4 Dimension of Country Evaluation

Figure 35, the following table, summarizes the 4 Dimensions of country evaluation. Note that Canada and Australia/New Zealand are included for comparison (currency used is U.S. $).

Country / Region	GDP Category & US$ GDP Per Person	# People	Total Software Market			English Language of Commerce?	Tech Sales & Buying Culture
			2010 ($ billion) – Tech. Adoption		2010-13 Forecasted Growth		
Singapore	Top $57,100 (3rd in world)	5 million	$ 1.1 advanced		7.7%	**Yes –** legislated language of business	• Only E. Asian country similar to U.S. and W. Europe in buying and business culture • Good supply of local tech talent, in strong demand with 2% unemployment • Hard to find qualified local Singaporean salespeople, tech companies usually resort to ex-patriots • Comparable compensation & employment costs to U.S.; forced retirement savings and personal income taxes are lower

Country / Region	GDP Category & US$ GDP Per Person	# People	Total Software Market			English Language of Commerce?	Tech Sales & Buying Culture
			2010 ($ billion) – Tech. Adoption	2010-13 Forecasted Growth			
Malaysia	Middle Income $14,900	28 million	$ 0.7 mid-level	8.4%		**Yes** for Chinese and Indian minorities and some Malay professionals **Probably no** for rest of Malays	• Challenging buying behavior and business culture, as legislation requires quota and majority ownership of native Malays. These practices slowly changing as the country modernizes • Reasonable supply of local tech talent in Chinese and Indians, in strong demand with unemployment < 4% • Hard to find qualified native Malaysian salespeople
Indonesia	Developing $4,300	238 million	$ 1.1 basic to mid-level	11.8%		**No**	• Challenging buying behavior, as the country modernizes from its corrupt past under the dictatorship ending in 1996 • Hard to find qualified local Indonesian tech talent
Sing.+ Malay.+ Indon.	$6,400	271 million	$ 2.9	9.4%			

Country / Region	GDP Category & US$ GDP Per Person	# People	Total Software Market			English Language of Commerce?	Tech Sales & Buying Culture
			2010 ($ billion)	Tech. Adoption	2010-13 Forecasted Growth		
China	Developing $7,300	1,335 million	$16.7 mid-level		12.3%	**No** – very little English spoken	• Radically dissimilar business culture and practices from N. America. Difficult for Western companies to establish Chinese company or subsidiary and enforce contracts • Non state-owned local companies (70% of GDP) disregard central government regulations: local regulators ignore this and no one sure which will be enforced. However, selective enforcement of laws favors local companies • Poor IP protection and market still developing
Hong Kong	Top $45,400	7 million	$ 0.5 advanced		7.6%	**Maybe, but probably no** • Cantonese is business language • Most speak Mandarin • 1/3 speak English, more than China or Taiwan	• Unique and singularly successful business culture: combination of the best of Chinese entrepreneurial and English rule of law, because its rapid growth and development occurred at the end of its 156 years as an English colony. Known as "East meets West" • Future is uncertain because of mainland Chinese takeover in 1997 and Chinese emphasizing Beijing and Shanghai as the business centers

Country / Region	GDP Category & US$ GDP Per Person	# People	Total Software Market			English Language of Commerce?	Tech Sales & Buying Culture
			2010 ($ billion) – Tech. Adoption		2010-13 Forecasted Growth		
Taiwan	Wealthy $35,500	23 million	$ 1.4 advanced		8.9%	**No** - very little English spoken	• Dissimilar business culture to U.S. and Europe, somewhat like China but more advanced and developed • Uncertain future, despite independence from China in 1949. China considers it a wayward territory
Greater China	Developing $7,985	1,365 million	$18.6		12.0%		
Japan	Wealthy $33,800	127 million	$14.2 advanced		4.1%	**No** - very little English spoken	• Distribution channels, business culture and practices unique, which Japanese prefer • Must sell through preferred channel partners demanded by large Japanese enterprises • Impossible to predict when software deal will close • Tech staff availability good, but very expensive, especially for English speakers • Necessary to have sales manager who can translate between Western and Japanese worlds

Country / Region	GDP Category & US$ GDP Per Person	# People	Total Software Market			English Language of Commerce?	Tech Sales & Buying Culture
			2010 ($ billion)	Tech. Adoption	2010-13 Forecasted Growth		
South Korea	Wealthy $30,000	48 million	$ 2.6 advanced		7.9%	**No** - little English spoken, but slightly more than Japan	• Similar to Japan, but not as extreme. Business practices are evolving to be more like the N. America and W. Europe. • Business conglomerates (chaebols) account for more than half of economy. Largest are led by multinationals (Samsung, LG, etc.). Selling to member is good reference for other members
Japan + South Korea	Wealthy $32,800	176 million	$ 16.9 advanced		4.7%		
India	Developing $3,400	1,194 million	$ 2.0 basic		11.5%	**Yes** – was English colony	• Local market challenging, as the vast majority of businesses are small and low-tech and the territory is large with poor transportation network • Import tariffs exist, government bureaucracy high • Price level very low: 10%–20% of U.S. and W. Europe level
TOTAL: E. Asia Top 9	$7,400	3,013 million	$ 40.4		9.0%		

Country / Region	GDP Category & US$ GDP Per Person	# People	Total Software Market			English Language of Commerce?	Tech Sales & Buying Culture
			2010 ($ billion)	Tech. Adoption	2010-13 Forecasted Growth		
Aus. + N. Z.	Wealthy $37,100	27.0 million	$4.4 advanced		7.0%	**Yes** – native	• Other than Canada, most similar to N. America in buying and business culture • Strong supply of sales & tech talent; developed, self-sufficient tech culture because of geographic isolation • Comparable compensation & higher employment costs than U.S.
Cana-da	Wealthy $38,800	34.3 million	$9.8 advanced		5.8%	Yes, except for Quebec with French	• Very close to U.S. in buying culture and similar business culture • Strong supply of sales & tech talent • Comparable compensation & higher employment costs than U.S.

Figure 35 – EAST ASIA: Summary of 4 Dimensions for Country Evaluation

Putting it All Together for East Asia

Taking all 4 Dimensions into account, Singapore is the best choice for most enterprise software vendors to initiate their expansion into East Asia. However, despite the presence of many multinationals who establish their Asian headquarters there, it has a tiny market of only five million people. It is close to Malaysia and Indonesia, both of which are modernizing and growing rapidly. Therefore, expanding market entry into these countries from a Singapore base increases the target market GDP by a factor of five and population from five million to 270 million. Despite Indonesia's population of more than 200 million, it is a challenging market for enterprise software:

- It is still a developing country

86

- It has a legacy of corrupt business practices
- English is not commonly spoken in the business community
- Not even close to the number of medium and enterprise businesses per capita as Singapore or Malaysia, which are the targets for enterprise software

After Singapore, Malaysia, and Indonesia, the southern part of East Asia, Japan and South Korea are usually the next targets for market entry because of their large GDPs, advanced economies with high technology acceptance, large number of enterprise and multinational companies, and many medium-sized companies that support the large organizations. However, both of these markets have business practices, cultures, and customs foreign to Westerners. They also have few English-speakers and selling enterprise software into these markets requires building partnerships with local companies. Both also require translation of enterprise software into their native languages, which are both double-byte languages.

Finally, after these markets are the giant, still developing, but rapidly growing subcontinents of India and China. Despite their enormous potential, sales operations in these markets are best initiated after enterprise software vendors have experience in the other two regions of East Asia.

5 LATIN AMERICA

Introduction

In this book, Latin America refers to the huge geographic area spanning Mexico, Central America, and South America. It excludes the Caribbean countries, which are grouped with the Rest of the World. Geographically, Mexico and Central America are part of North America.

Figure 36, a map depicting Latin America, follows:

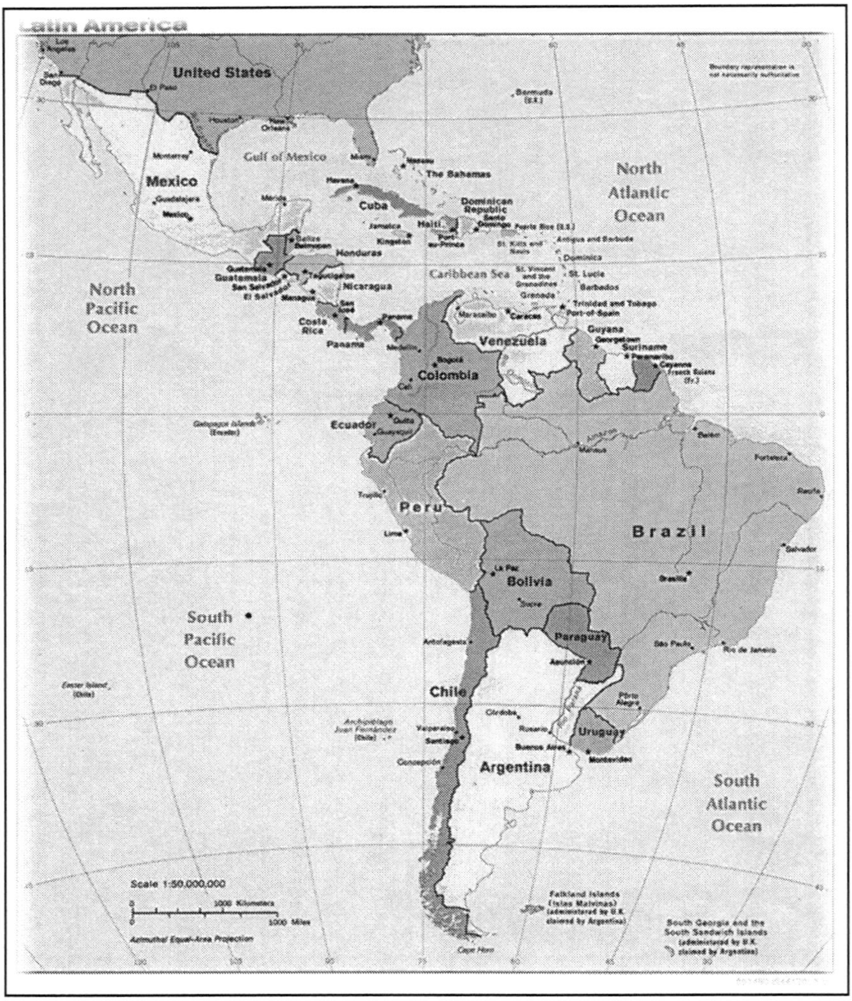

Figure 36 – Map of Latin America

Latin America has traditionally been one of the poorer areas in the world with anti-business, populist governments that have hindered the growth of its economies. It has had some of the widest income disparities in the world, with profound implications for selling enterprise software:

1. Technology is affordable only to a chosen few.

2. The small and medium business formation rate is low. Those that do exist tend to be low tech and often don't invest enterprise technology.

3. An inordinate percentage of the GDP is dominated by large enterprises owned by a few rich families or governmental institutions.

Latin American countries' investment rate is low compared to other parts of the world. The few rich families tend not to invest their wealth locally, due to historically weak currencies. Many skirt the laws restricting the direct export of funds by investing in real estate outside their countries, such as in Miami or Los Angeles.

However, this bleak economic picture for Latin America has changed suddenly over the last decade with the emergence of stronger, more democratic governments that have fostered confidence and the emergence of more and higher quality businesses. Nevertheless, individual Latin American countries run the risk of falling into dysfunction by quasi-dictators, such as Hugo Chavez in Venezuela, coming into power. A weak government also enables situations to spin out of control, such as the war being waged by the Mexican drug cartels or Argentina's default on its international debt.

The Latin American countries tend to be wary of each other, despite being connected by the common language of Spanish (except for Brazilians, who speak Portuguese). In the recent past, Latin American countries have not conquered and occupied each other, as in East Asia, but they are not as close to each other as the Europeans, who have joined into the economic and quasi-governmental European Union. The Latin Americans have half-heartedly attempted to form free-trade alliances and economic organizations. Most notable of these is Mercosur, which is a free-trade area consisting of Brazil, Argentina, Uruguay, and Paraguay. However, it hasn't expanded beyond these four countries. Culturally, the variation between Latin American countries is low, more similar to Europe than East Asia.

There are large distances separating the countries and huge natural barriers, such as the Amazon rainforest (by far the largest in the world) and the Andes mountain range, which separates the South American continent from North to South, a distance of more than 4,000 miles. Perhaps due to these large distances and rugged geography, no city in Latin America has emerged as a multi-country business hub. Miami is really the business capital of Latin America, with the security of the U.S. dollar, its comparatively stable real-estate values, widespread Latin American culture, and many Spanish and

Portuguese-speaking residents. Miami is a great location for a multi-country Latin American sales office because of its characteristics.

Latin America: Wealth

Figure 37 illustrates comparative GDP PPP and population of Latin American countries:

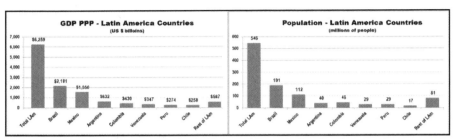

Figure 37 – LATIN AMERICA: GDP PPP and Population by Country

The graphs in **Figure 37** show that the three largest Latin American countries—Brazil, Mexico, Argentina—stand out in GDP and population size. The size of the economies and population falls off drastically after these three.

Figure 38 shows 2010 GDP PPP and population data for the top eight Latin American economies ranked by size. The three largest Latin American countries, which account for more than two-thirds of total Latin America GDP, are highlighted with gray stripes:

GDP Rank		GDP using PPP (US $ billions)			Population (millions)				GDP (PPP) / Person		
		World Rank	US$ (billion)	% of LAm	% of World	World Rank	People (millions)	% of LAm	% of World	US $	LAm Rank	(LAm = 100)
1.	Brazil	7	2,181	34.8%	2.9%	5	190.7	34.9%	2.8%	11,437	5	100
2.	Mexico	11	1,550	24.8%	2.1%	11	112.3	20.6%	1.6%	13,802	3	120
3.	Argentina	22	632	10.1%	0.9%	32	40.1	7.3%	0.6%	15,761	1	137
4.	Colombia	28	430	6.9%	0.6%	28	45.9	8.4%	0.7%	9,368	6	82
5.	Venezuela	34	347	5.5%	0.5%	42	29.1	5.3%	0.4%	11,924	4	104
6.	Peru	41	274	4.4%	0.4%	40	29.4	5.4%	0.4%	9,320	7	81
7.	Chile	43	258	4.1%	0.3%	60	17.1	3.1%	0.2%	15,088	2	132
8.	Ecuador	64	114	1.8%	0.2%	68	14.3	2.6%	0.2%	7,972	8	70
TOTAL - L. Amer.			$ 6,259		8.5%		546		7.9%	$ 11,465		100

Figure 38 – LATIN AMERICA: Top 8 Economies Ranked by 2010 GDP[xxxiv]

92

Figure 39 recasts the list of Latin America countries from highest to lowest by 2010 GDP PPP per person:

GDP Rank		World Rank	GDP using PPP (US $ billions)			World Rank	Population (millions)			GDP (PPP) / Person		
			US$ (billion)	% of LAm	% of World		People (millions)	% of LAm	% of World	US $	LAm Rank	(LAm = 100)
3.	Argentina	22	632	10.1%	0.9%	32	40.1	7.3%	0.6%	15,761	1	137
7.	Chile	43	258	4.1%	0.3%	60	17.1	3.1%	0.2%	15,088	2	132
2.	Mexico	11	1,550	24.8%	2.1%	11	112.3	20.6%	1.6%	13,802	3	120
5.	Venezuela	34	347	5.5%	0.5%	42	29.1	5.3%	0.4%	11,924	4	104
1.	Brazil	7	2,181	34.8%	2.9%	5	190.7	34.9%	2.8%	11,437	5	100
4.	Colombia	28	430	6.9%	0.6%	28	45.9	8.4%	0.7%	9,368	6	82
6.	Peru	41	274	4.4%	0.4%	40	29.4	5.4%	0.4%	9,320	7	81
8.	Ecuador	64	114	1.8%	0.2%	68	14.3	2.6%	0.2%	7,972	8	70
TOTAL - L. Amer.			$ 6,259		8.5%		546		7.9%	$ 11,465		100

Figure 39 – LATIN AMERICA: 2010 GDP per Person, Ranked from Highest to Lowest

Compared to the countries in Europe or East Asia, the range of GDP PPP per person in the Latin American countries is in a narrower band. The top five Latin American countries by GDP per person are in the *Middle Income* category of GDP per person.

The data above doesn't illustrate the huge income inequality between the top and bottom earners in Latin America, the largest gap in the world.[xxxv] This stunts growth in Latin America as only a few wealthy families control huge swaths of the entrenched economies. A low percentage of the population is middle class, which in most of the world accounts for the bulk of a country's consumption. Business formation has traditionally been low outside the small, privileged classes, meaning the enterprise software markets are limited to a small number of enterprise organizations, many of which are inefficient state-owned enterprise such as national banks, oil companies, and the governments themselves.

The top three countries in Latin America (Brazil, Mexico and Argentina), together encompass 70% of total Latin American GDP. Because of their size relative to the remaining countries, they stand out as the obvious choice for enterprise software companies to consider market entry. Chile is added to this group by virtue of its economic success. Chile and Argentina are adjacent to each other and their business capitals are only a few hours apart by plane, despite being separated by the formidable Andes mountain range.

- **Brazil**

In 2010, Brazil was the seventh largest economy in the world in terms of GDP PPP and is poised to pass Russia for sixth place in 2011. Its large population, capacity for rapid development, effective government policies, and abundant natural resources has propelled it to become a regional superpower with a growing world presence:

- Brazil's natural resources, including the Amazon River, its vast river basin of almost three million square miles, and the largest rainforest in the world offer huge development possibilities, effective government policies, somewhat tempered by the world's growing "green" consciousness against rainforest destruction. Also, one of the largest oil discoveries worldwide in the last 50 years was in the deep water off the Brazilian coast. Brazil will become an OPEC member once it starts oil production from this discovery.

- Brazil has the fifth largest population in the world and continues to grow rapidly. Its culture is racially diverse and multicultural.

- Over the last fifteen years, the Brazilian economy has rapidly expanded, and its currency has stabilized for the first time in its modern history. Its current president is the second leader in a row with supposedly anti-business, populist credentials, but she has continued a surprisingly pro-business trend and oversees economic policy that has continued to sustain Brazil's rapid economic ascent.

Brazil's standing in the world and its diplomatic power is increasing, but it still does not have as much influence as its economic and natural resources might indicate. However, it is a leader in the non-aligned country movement, and alongside China, is one of co-leaders of the "BRICS" countries (Brazil, Russia, India, China, South Africa), an informal organization of large developing countries "of similar stage of newly advanced economic development."[xxxvi] Brazil will also host the Olympics in 2016 and the Soccer World Cup in 2014, the two largest sporting events in the world and both firsts for South America. Clearly, Brazil's political and international influence is on the rise.

Despite all its advantages and growing influence, entering the Brazilian market remains difficult, which is hounded by protectionism and mind-numbing regulations. Crime driven by the wide income disparity remains a problem for both Sao Paulo and Rio de Janeiro, the two major economic areas accounting for more than half of Brazilian GDP. Brazil's language is Portuguese, unique to Brazil and Portugal. However, Brazil is a rapidly emerging nation, and enterprise software vendors will be missing out by not overcoming the barriers to launch their sales in this market.

- **Mexico**

The economy of Mexico has come to depend on participation in the North American Free Trade Agreement and energy production, which waxes and wanes with cyclical demand and changing prices. Up until the mid-2000s, its economy was on an upward trajectory with free market reforms, and the corrupt political system was showing the first signs of change after a peaceful ousting of the single political party that had been in power since Mexico's independence in 1910.

However, Mexican progress has reversed as it faces problems related to illicit drugs, which has escalated into a war between the government and the powerful drug cartels. Demand for drugs is stoked by insatiable demand from its neighbor to the north, the U.S. The Mexican government has cracked down on drug cartels, and the cartels are fighting back, which is hurting international business and upsetting everyday life in Mexico. The country's murder total exceeds 20,000 annually in a country with one-third the population of the U.S. Kidnapping of Mexican government officials, businessman, and wealthy family scions is a persistent problem on the rise in Mexico. This crime has now spread to non-Mexican businesspeople, which does not bode well for expansion into Mexico for enterprise software vendors and other businesses. Mexican medium and enterprise organizations are nervous about their country and are reluctant to consider technology investments such as enterprise software. Until this crime problem associated with drug cartels is minimized, Mexico will not be a good locale for enterprise software vendors to consider for expansion.

- **Argentina**

It is often noted that Argentina had one of the world's largest GDPs in 1910, but since then it has become a minor player in the world. Its influence is waning within Latin America as well. Argentina does have the highest GDP per person in Latin America, slightly ahead of Mexico and Chile, but its economic progress has declined since an economic and political crisis at the end of 2001 resulted in the country defaulting on its international debt. The

Argentine peso, which had been tied to the U.S. dollar, was crippled by devaluation. Three presidents came and went within two weeks. Argentina has still not fully recovered from these economic and governmental crises. The number of medium and enterprise organizations in Argentina is limited in an economy one-third the size of Mexico. Argentine businesses and organizations won't widely consider new technology investments in such an uncertain economic environment. For these reasons, Argentina is not currently a good target for expansion.

- **Chile**

Chile was the first country to emerge from the weak economic and governmental legacy of Latin America in the early 1970s, after its dictator departed. This country of seventeen million people started free-market economic reforms that set it on the path to becoming one of the most prosperous countries in the Western Hemisphere, and its success has been bolstered by a Free Trade Agreement with the U.S. since 2004.

Despite its sizable economic progress over the last forty years, this is a country approximately one-tenth the size of Brazil. An enterprise software vendor who initiates Latin America expansion in Brazil and Mexico typically expands into Chile and Argentina simultaneously, as the two countries are adjacent and together are approximately one-half the size of Mexico.

Latin America: Acceptance of Technology

The four Latin America countries above are similar for technology acceptance, which is not surprising considering they have similar GDPs per person and all of them have the similar problem of uneven income distribution endemic to Latin America. As was outlined above, this hinders economic growth and company formation, limiting technology acceptance.

Figure 40 examines measures of technology acceptance, summarizes wealth and lists total software market sizes and Internet usage as a percent of the total population for the four largest Latin America economies. It is sorted by software market size and the U.S. and Canada are added for reference.

Country	GDP per Person / Total GDP	# People (million)	Total Software Market		Internet Users		
			2010 Total / Tech Adoption	2010-13 Forecasted Growth	Actual (million)	World Rank	% of People
U.S.	$46,900 $14,630 billion	312	$130.0 bill. advanced	5.4%	240	2	77%
Brazil	$11,400 $ 2,180 billion	191	$ 2.8 billion mid-level	6.4%	76	5	40%
Mexico	$13,800 $ 1,550 billion	112	$ 1.4 billion mid-level	9.1%	31	14	27%
Argen-tina	$15,800 $ 630 billion	40	$ 0.4 billion mid-level	11.8%	27	19	66%
Chile	$15,100 $ 260 billion	17	$ 0.3 billion mid-level	8.9%	8	36	49%
Canada	$38,800 $ 1,330 billion	34	$ 9.8 billion advanced	5.8%	26	12	76%
Latin Amer. Top 4	$12,800 $ 4,620 billion	360	$ 4.9 billion all mid-level	7.8%	142		39%

Figure 40 – LATIN AMERICA: GDP, Population, Total Software Markets[x], Internet Usage[xi]

Figure 40 illustrates that the Internet usage rates for the Latin American countries average 40% of the population. This is similar to the upper end of middle-income markets such as Turkey, which is at a similar stage of development and GDP per person as the Latin American countries. Using these measures as a proxy for technology acceptance implies the Latin American propensity to embrace technology is below the *Wealthy* and *Top*

GDP per person of the rich countries and more similar to the middle-income countries of Turkey and South Africa. Consequently, the business case for enterprise software vendors is not as strong for market entry in Latin America as it is for the higher income countries such as the large economies of Europe, Australia, New Zealand, Japan, Korea, or Singapore.

Figure 41 illustrates 2010 software market sizes and 2010-2013 forecasted growth rates for Latin America, along with Canada and the U.S. added for reference. It also shows percentages of regional and world totals:

Country	2010 Total Software Market ($ billions)	Software Market % of Total		2010 – 2013 Forecasted Growth	2013 Forecast	
		% Latin America	% World		Total Software Market ($ billions)	% World
U.S.	$130.0	> 22x	40.0%	5.4%	$152.0	37.2%
Brazil	$ 2.8	48.4%	0.9%	6.4%	$ 3.4	0.8%
Mexico	$ 1.4	23.3%	0.4%	9.1%	$ 1.8	0.4%
Argentina	$ 0.4	7.2%	0.1%	11.8%	$ 0.6	0.1%
Chile	$ 0.3	5.6%	0.1%	8.9%	$ 0.4	0.1%
Canada	$ 9.8	169.0%	3.0%	5.8%	$11.6	2.8%
Latin America Top 4	$ 5.8	84.5%	1.5%	7.8%	$ 6.2	1.4%

Figure 41 – LATIN AMERICA: 2010-2013 Total Software Market Sizes, Growth Rates, % of Total Region & World

Brazil's relatively low forecasted annual software growth for 2010-2013 of 6.4% reduces the overall Latin American growth forecast to 7.8% annually. This is lower than Europe and East Asia's forecasted 2010-2013 annual growth rates of 10.1% and 9.0% respectively and even below the world baseline rate of 8%.

Looking next at the total Latin American software markets graphically, **Figure 42** compares the total software market sizes by country to GDP PPP by country for the four major Latin America economies and the Rest of Latin America:

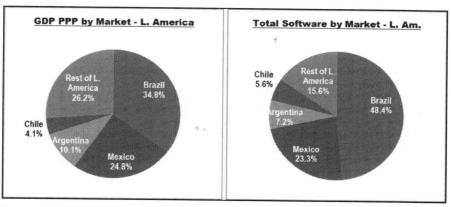

Figure 42 – Top Latin America Economies: GDP vs. Total Software Market Sizes

Figure 43 ranks the Latin America software markets by comparison of the country's share of total Latin American software to share of total Latin American GDP. The higher the rank and index, the more desirable the country is for enterprise software sales:

Country	% of Total Latin America			Software Sales as % of GDP
	Software Market Size	GDP PPP	Index (see footnote xxxvii)	
Brazil	48.4%	34.8%	139	0.15%
Chile	5.6%	4.1%	137	0.18%
Mexico	23.3%	24.8%	94	0.15%
Argentina	7.2%	10.1%	71	0.14%
Latin America: Top 4	84.5%	73.8%	114	0.13%

Figure 43 – LATIN AMERICA: Comparison of GDP Share to Total Software Market Share

Brazil and Chile have the largest software markets compared to their share of Latin American GDP. Latin America countries have a lower percentage of their GDP attributable to software than other parts of the world: the U.S. ratio is close to 1% and the top markets of Europe have software percentages of total GDP ranging from Benelux at 1.18% to the UK at 2.26%. The U.S. share of GDP attributable to software is 0.88%.

Another approach to assessing technology acceptance across countries is the World Economic Forum's network readiness index (NRI), which was described directly before **Figure 7** on page 20 and a custom index to measure "readiness to embrace to enterprise software" on the same scale: 1 (low) to 7 (high). Illustrated below in **Figure 44** are the NRI and custom index results for Latin America and other selected countries:

	NRI Index					Custom Index: Enterprise Software (Scale of 1 to 7, low to high)							
						12.5%	22.5%	12.5%	15.0%	12.5%	25.0%	100%	
	Index Score (1-7, LO-HI)	World Rank: '10-'11	Change: '10→'11	World Rank: '06-'07	Change: '07→'11	Avail. Of Latest Tech.	Laws Relating to ICT	Avail. - Scientists & Eng.	Buyer Sophistication	Extent of Staff Training	Co. Level of Tech. Absorp.	CUSTOM INDEX	CUSTOM INDEX, Brazil = 100
Latin America													
Chile	4.28	39	1	31	-8	6.0	5.0	4.9	4.1	4.4	5.3	4.98	109
Brazil	3.90	56	5	53	-3	5.5	4.5	4.0	3.6	4.2	5.2	4.57	100
Mexico	3.69	78	0	49	-29	4.9	3.9	3.8	3.3	3.8	4.5	4.06	89
Argentina	3.47	96	-5	63	-33	4.7	3.1	4.0	3.5	3.8	4.4	3.89	85
Colombia	3.89	58	2	64	6	4.7	4.2	3.8	3.4	3.6	4.5	4.09	90
Peru	3.54	89	3	78	-11	5.1	3.8	3.6	3.5	3.8	4.8	4.14	91
Venezuela	3.16	119	-7	83	-36	4.3	2.9	3.4	3.2	3.7	4.2	3.61	79
Selected Other Countries													
U.S.	5.33	5	0	7	2	6.4	5.4	5.7	4.5	5.1	6.0	5.54	121
Canada	5.21	8	-1	11	3	6.4	5.5	5.6	4.7	5.0	5.6	5.47	120
Australia	5.06	17	-1	15	-2	6.1	5.5	4.5	4.4	4.8	5.9	5.30	116
India	4.03	48	-5	44	-4	5.6	4.5	5.2	3.8	4.1	5.3	4.77	104
China	4.35	36	1	59	23	4.4	4.4	4.6	4.6	4.1	4.9	4.54	100
Turkey	3.79	71	-2	52	-19	5.5	4.3	4.5	2.9	3.7	5.1	4.39	96
Israel	4.81	22	6	18	-4	6.4	4.5	5.1	3.4	4.7	6.1	5.07	111
S. Africa	3.86	61	1	47	-14	5.5	4.8	3.3	4.1	4.7	5.4	4.73	104
Indonesia	3.92	53	14	62	9	4.8	3.9	4.7	3.9	4.4	4.9	4.43	97

Figure 44 – LATIN AMERICA: NRI and Custom Enterprise Software Readiness Index

The custom "readiness to embrace enterprise software" index shows Chile and Brazil as the highest in Latin America at 4.98 and 4.57, which is similar to China and India and other mid-sized emerging countries such as Israel, South Africa, and Indonesia. However, these scores are significantly below the advanced countries of the U.S., Canada, and Australia, which range from 5.30 to 5.44.

The decline in country rank of NRI scores over the last four years for the four largest Latin American countries is a worrying trend: Chile and Brazil eight and three places, respectively, and Mexico and Argentina declining even more, twenty-nine and thirty-three places. This is to be expected for Mexico and Argentina, with the depth of governmental and economic crises that each of them is facing. More surprising are the declines for Chile and Brazil, whose economic progress has continued unabated over these years. Perhaps their advances in information and communications technology are just occurring slower than in many of the other countries surveyed for the NRI analysis.

Summary of Wealth and Technology Acceptance

To summarize the *Wealth* and *Acceptance of Technology* sections, the top three economies of Latin America (Brazil, Mexico, and Argentina) plus successful Chile account for almost 75% of Latin American GDP. All are at a roughly similar stage of development, with Brazil having the growth, size, resources, and pro-business government to become a world power with a rapidly expanding base of medium and enterprise businesses hungry to invest in new technology. As for Chile, despite its small size—4% of Latin American GDP—it is continuing along its growth trajectory, and there is no reason to believe its success won't continue. Both Mexico and Argentina (roughly 25% and 10% of Latin American GDP, respectively) are in economic stagnation:

- **Mexico** – its war with the drug cartels is causing widespread violence and terror throughout the country

- **Argentina** – it has not yet recovered from a ten-year economic crisis that began when the country defaulted on its international debt and its currency went into a free fall

Technology acceptance in the three large Latin American countries plus Chile is at similar levels: less than the advanced economies of U.S., Canada, the UK, and Australia, but similar to other middle-income countries such as Turkey and South Africa. Note that Argentina has a slightly higher Internet usage rate than the other Latin American counties, similar to Italy and Spain. The total Latin America software market is small with the top three markets plus Chile approximately 60% the size of Canada. Compared to the advanced economies of the U.S. and Europe, the Latin American medium and growing organizations that are the target markets for enterprise software are not as attractive prospects as the same entities might be in the advanced economies. Although there are fewer enterprise businesses than in the advanced countries, Latin American enterprise organizations in such industries as financial services, energy, and government are the top targets for enterprise software.

Latin America: Acceptance of English as a Language for Commerce

As outlined in the previous sections, English as the language for commerce is crucial when considering market entry for enterprise software sales, because it is by far the most widely spoken language in technology. Assuming that most enterprise software is initially written in English, many start their international expansion in the English-speaking countries and those where English is widely spoken and understood in the business world. This enables the cost of translating the software into other languages to be deferred until the software vendor has an opportunity to gain international field experience to better understand the required order of other languages.

All Latin American countries are Spanish-speaking except Brazil, where Portuguese is spoken. In terms of GDP and population for all of Latin America, this breaks down to approximately two-thirds Spanish and one-third Portuguese. Considering Brazil, Mexico, Argentina, and Chile as a unit, Brazil encompasses approximately half of both GDP and population of the total of these four countries.

Spanish and Portuguese translations are required for selling enterprise software in Latin America, except for a small number of software products targeted toward enterprise data centers, which can get by in English at first. Web sites and marketing materials will need to be translated into Spanish and Portuguese.

Latin America: The Technology Sales and Buying Culture

As described previously, this measure is based on the similarity of the market's technology evaluation and buying practices to those of the U.S. and the large economies of Europe. Being the dominant markets for enterprise software, these territories are chosen as benchmarks. Additionally, part of assessing the technology sales and buying culture is the all-important availability of qualified people to staff the international sales operation start-up. The most important functions at the beginning are:

1. **Sales Staff** – Those who can sell directly as well as through channels;

2. **Technical Staff** – Those having strong people skills for presales support, for training channel partners, and having knowledge of the technical aspects of consultative sales.

The Technology Sales and Buying Cultures are similar across the three large Latin American countries plus Chile, with Brazil being the slight outlier because of its preponderance of business regulations. The Latin American sales and buying cultures are more similar to each other than European countries are to one another, and these four Latin American countries are also at a similar stage of development and technology acceptance. This common sales and buying culture across Latin American is more different from North America than the UK, Northern Europe, Germany, and France. However, it is approximately the same degree of difference from North America as Spain and Italy (see **Europe: The Technology Sales and Buying Culture**, starting on page 36). Not surprisingly, Latin American countries were colonies of Spain and Portugal until the late nineteenth and early twentieth centuries. However, the Latin American sales and buying cultures and business processes for organizations deciding on major technology purchases are more like North America than the East Asian countries, except for Singapore (see **East Asia: The Technology Sales and Buying Culture** starting on page 70).

The following sections present the aspects of the sales and buying cultures of the countries that differ from the Latin America norm. The availability of technology and sales staff for enterprise software sales is also discussed. Note that many enterprise software vendors locate their Latin American sales headquarters in Miami instead of in South America. Miami has a strong supply of Spanish and Portuguese-speakers for staffing software sales and technology positions. It also has frequent flight connections to the major business capitals in Latin America. Finally, placing headquarters in Miami eliminates jealousy engendered by selection of one country over another. However, Brazil is now big enough to have its own sales office from the outset of expansion into Latin America.

1. Brazil – *Mid-Level* Technology Adoption

Despite its unlimited potential, the sales and buying culture in Brazil is the most difficult in Latin America. There are a myriad of regulations for setting up and operating a business, even more so for a foreign company. This has made the Brazil business environment ripe for corruption, as poorly paid bureaucrats can extort money from foreign companies to get an official stamp on a business document. Doing business in Brazil has been compared to India, although Brazil is not as extreme as India with regards to bureaucracy.

The same bureaucratic approach permeates Brazilian organizations considering purchase of enterprise software. Even when a large organization has decided to purchase enterprise software, completing a business transaction requires many stamps and approvals, which are processed by low-level administrative staff. Brazil has erected protectionist barriers against non-Brazilian manufactured goods in order to establish its own manufacturing industry, but this has not directly affected software exports to Brazil. However, sometimes buyers exhibit a negative attitude toward non-Brazilian products. At this point in time, there is not much of a home-grown Brazilian software industry. But, with widespread Internet availability, the large population of young people addicted to electronics and social networking, and new software delivery paradigms, who is to know if some of the next software geniuses will come from Brazil?

Brazil's foreign business culture and the need for fluent Portuguese speakers require hiring local Brazilian sales management early in the evolution of market expansion into Brazil. Native sales management will have insight into the arcane business laws and be able to translate the Brazilian enterprise software sales cycles into something a North American can understand. Recognizing sales talent in Brazil also requires local management. The compensation for such a local Brazilian sales manager, fluent in English, who can bridge the Brazilian and North American business cultures, is higher than most locales in Latin America and is starting to rival Europe and Japan.

Technical talent to support an enterprise software vendor's Brazilian sales operation is more widely available in Brazil than other parts of Latin America. However, finding English-speaking technical staff requires paying premium salaries.

2. Mexico – *Mid-Level* Technology Adoption

Before the modernization started by the most recent government in Mexico, doing business there was difficult for any American company trying not to violate the U.S. Foreign Corrupt Practices Act (i.e. not bribing to close sales). The preferred approach was selling through channel partners that could mask this unsavory practice to close deals. The Mexican government has legislated reforms that have made Mexican business practices closer to the rest of Latin America. However, all of this came to a screeching halt when the war against drug cartels brought severe violence into everyday Mexican life.

Mexico has uneven income distribution issues like other Latin American countries, namely the top few percent of income earners earn a disproportionate percentage of the total income of the country. Because of the small middle class, business formation is low, and there is a dearth of rapid growth medium-sized companies. Mexico has a high percentage of its enterprise businesses controlled by the government and a few rich families. That ownership structure accounts for huge swaths of the economy including industries such as mobile phones, retail, media, banking, and oil production. These few giant enterprises are the primary target prospects for enterprise software.

3. Argentina and Chile – *Mid-Level* Technology Adoption

If and when Argentina puts its economy and government in order, the sales and buying culture will be similar to Mexico and the rest of Latin America. There is a strong argument for managing Argentina from Miami or through channel partners at first, because its size might not justify a local sales office.

Chile, despite its economic success, is too small for most enterprise software vendors to justify a local sales office. This can be mitigated by initiating the management of both the Chilean and Argentine sales efforts from Miami. When increasing revenue justifies a local sales presence, both of these countries can be managed from Argentina.

The leading industries for technology spending for the top countries of Latin America are illustrated in **Figure 45** just below. It compares the breakdown of total technology spending by industry for the top three Latin America economies plus Chile:

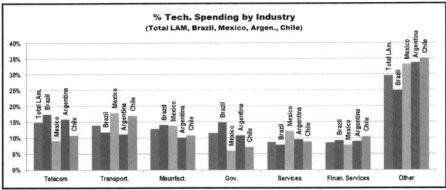

Figure 45 – LATIN AMERICA: Total Technology Spending[xxii] by Leading Industry Segments

The country segments for total technology spending that stand out for their differences are:

- **Mexico and Chile, Telecom** spending – lower than the other Latin American countries at approximately 10% of total technology spending, whereas the other countries are approximately 15%.

- **Brazil, Government** spending – at 15% of total technology spending in Brazil, higher than anywhere else.

4. The Rest of Latin America

Outside Brazil, Mexico, Argentina, and small prosperous Chile, the only other sizeable markets in Latin America are Colombia and Venezuela (each approximately one-half to two-thirds the size of Argentina), and Peru (approximately the size of Chile but much poorer). None are worthy targets to initiate market entry for enterprise software:

- Colombia and Peru are *Developing*, the lowest category of GDP per person, and are politically unstable. However, both are improving.

- Venezuela has a slightly larger GDP per person than the others in this group, just into the *Middle Income* category. It has large oil reserves, but is being ravaged by a dictator who has tampered with the constitution, nationalized many industries including banks, oil production, power generation and now gold mining. He is rumored to be looting government reserves.

There are thirteen additional tiny countries in Latin America, each with GDPs of US $100 billion or less—all too small and poor for a typical enterprise software vendor to consider market entry. The combined GDP of these countries is approximately US $600 billion, and their combined population totals 81 million—less than 15% of the total population of Latin America.

When an enterprise software vendor has international sales operations serving Brazil, Mexico, Argentina, and Chile and is ready to gain access to Colombia, Peru, and Venezuela, a typical model would be a regional sales office in Miami supported by channel partners in those countries.

Latin America: Summary – Results from 4 Dimensions of Country Evaluation

Figure 46, the following table, summarizes the 4 Dimensions of country evaluation for Latin America. Canada is added for comparison purposes (currency used is U.S. $):

Country / Region	GDP Category & US$ GDP Per Person	# People	Total Software Market			English for Language of Commerce?	Tech Sales & Buying Culture
			2010 ($ billion) – Tech. Adoption	2010-13 Forecasted Growth			
Brazil	Middle Income $11,400	191 million	$ 2.6 mid-level	6.4%		**No –** need Portu-guese	• Most dissimilar Latin American buying and business culture to N. America. Very bureaucratic and many regulations for operating a business • Sufficient supply of tech talent, but English-speaking difficult to find • Must pay a premium for local sales manager to bridge Brazilian and N. American culture and language

Country / Region	GDP Category & US$ GDP Per Person	# People	Total Software Market			English for Language of Commerce?	Tech Sales & Buying Culture
			2010 ($ billion) / Tech. Adoption	2010-13 Forecasted Growth			
Mexico	Middle Income $13,800	112 million	$ 1.4 mid-level	9.1%		**No –** need Spanish	• Similar buying behavior to rest of Latin America: more different from N. America than the UK, Northern Europe, Germany, and France. Approximately the same degree of difference from N. America as Spain and Italy • War with drug cartels makes Mexico dangerous for non-Mexicans. Not suitable for market entry at this time, but can start with channel partners managed from Miami
Argentina	Middle Income $15,800	40 million	$ 0.4 mid-level	11.8%		**No –** need Spanish	• Similar buying behavior to rest of Latin America: more different from N. America than the UK, Northern Europe, Germany, and France. Approximately the same degree of difference from N. America as Spain and Italy • Slightly higher Internet usage rates and broadband penetration than the rest of Latin America • Governmental turmoil and economic problems remain since early 2000 default on international debt. Not suitable for market entry at this time but can start with channel partners managed from Miami

Country / Region	GDP Category & US$ GDP Per Person	# People	Total Software Market			English for Language of Commerce?	Tech Sales & Buying Culture
			2010 ($ billion)	Tech. Adoption	2010-13 Forecasted Growth		
Chile	Middle Income $15,100	17 million	$ 0.3 mid-level		8.9%	No – need Spanish	• Similar buying behavior to rest of Latin America: more different from N. America than the UK, Northern Europe, Germany, and France. Approximately the same degree of difference from N. America as Spain and Italy • Prosperous and well-run economy • Begin market entry from Miami, then start in-country sales managed from Argentina as Argentina improves
Colombia	Developing $9,300	46 million	$ 0.3 basic		9.3%	No – need Spanish	• Buying behavior further away from N. America with anti-business sentiment and governments more overbearing • Too small and poor to consider for market entry at this time. Could manage sales through channel partners in Miami • Venezuela – "Dictator for life" in place • Colombia, Peru – intermittent political and economic instability
Venezuela	Middle Income $11,900	29 million	$ 0.3 mid-level		9.5%		
Peru	Developing $9,300	29 million	$ 0.2 basic		9.6%		
Rest of Latin America	Developing $7,200	81 million	$0.2 basic		9.1%	No – need Spanish	• 13 tiny and poor countries. After sales initiated into the rest of Latin America, sales from regional offices in Miami through channel partners

Country / Region	GDP Category & US$ GDP Per Person	# People	Total Software Market			English for Language of Commerce?	Tech Sales & Buying Culture
			2010 ($ billion) – Tech. Adoption		2010-13 Forecasted Growth		
Canada	Wealthy $38,800	34.3 million	$9.8 advanced		5.8%	**Yes**, except for Quebec with French	• Very close to U.S. in buying culture and similar business culture • Strong supply of sales & tech talent • Comparable compensation & higher employment costs than U.S.

Figure 46 – LATIN AMERICA: Summary of 4 Dimensions for Country Evaluation

Putting It All Together for Latin America

When all 4 dimensions are taken into account, Brazil stands out as the best market in Latin America for a typical enterprise software vendor to initiate expansion into this part of the world. This is tempered by the difficulty of doing business in Brazil, the requirement to translate software into Portuguese, and the need to hire a local sales manager who can translate between the business worlds of North America and Brazil. Despite these challenges, an enterprise software vendor cannot afford to miss out on the potentially huge and growing Brazilian market.

Once sales are underway in Brazil, an enterprise software vendor faces a quandary. The next two most desirable markets, Mexico and Argentina, are hobbled by internal problems: Mexico has startling crime from its war with the drug cartels; and Argentina has not recovered from ten years ago, when it defaulted on its international debt. Neither is suitable for market entry at this time. Chile, with only 17 million people (40% of the size of Argentina), is economically healthy and progressive, but it is too small for a direct sales presence of its own. The best approach after starting in Brazil is to initiate sales into Mexico, Argentina, and Chile from Miami using channel partners. Once Argentina stabilizes, then it and Chile can be started simultaneously from an office in Argentina.

Next come Venezuela, Colombia, and Peru—all too poor, not high enough technology acceptance, nor enough medium and enterprise entities to justify market entry.

6 CANADA, AUSTRALIA, NEW ZEALAND

Introduction

The remaining countries are a mix of various sizes and levels of development and are not contiguous, which means no economies of scale are gained by entering groups of markets close to each other. To analyze the remaining countries through the lens of enterprise software vendor market entry, the three English-speaking and wealthy countries of Canada, Australia, and New Zealand are lumped together, and the rest of the world is taken as a whole in the next chapter, the "Rest of the World" on page 123.

Canada, Australia and New Zealand

Despite these countries not being contiguous, they are very similar in their wealth profiles, technology acceptance, and technology sales and buying cultures, with the added bonus that all three are native English-speaking countries. They are grouped together because of these similarities, including the approach a typical enterprise software vendor would take to enter these markets.

From the standpoint of an enterprise software vendor starting up sales, Canada can be considered an extension of the U.S. because of its cultural similarity and location directly north of the U.S. Its border with the U.S. is the longest continuous border between any two countries in the world.

Australia and New Zealand (A/NZ) can be considered as a single unit. Even though these two independent countries are separated by 1,200 miles of ocean, they are relatively close considering they are the most remote inhabited large landmasses in the world. Their cultures are similar, and they have a strong trading relationship with each other. However, New Zealand is sensitive to being dominated by its larger neighbor, not dissimilar from the U.S. and Canada. Australia and New Zealand actually have more in common than the U.S. and Canada: contrast the friendly, sensitive Canadians with the more raucous, sometimes bullying U.S. Both Australia and New Zealand have low population densities (more sheep than people in both places) with large distances between their major business centers.

Canada, Australia, and New Zealand: Wealth and Technology Acceptance

Figure 47 lists 2010 GDPs using PPP and populations of the three countries:

	GDP using PPP (US $ billions)			Population (millions)			GDP (PPP) / Person	
	World Rank	US$ (billion)	% of World	World Rank	People (millions)	% of World	US $	Index (E. Asia = 100)
Australia / NZ								
Australia	17	882	1.2%	50	22.6	0.3%	$ 39,027	587
New Zealand	61	120	0.2%	123	4.4	0.1%	$ 27,273	410
TOTAL - Aus. / NZ		$ 1,002	1.4%		27.0	0.4%	$ 37,111	558
Canada	14	1,330	1.8%	35	34.3	0.5%	$ 38,776	583
TOTAL - Canada, A/NZ		$ 2,332	3.2%		61.3		$ 38,042	572

Figure 47 – CANADA, AUSTRALIA, NEW ZEALAND: 2010 GDPs and Populations

The three countries combined are approximately the size of the second largest economies in Europe: the UK plus Ireland or France.

Canada and Australia's GDPs per person are in the *Wealthy* range with New Zealand slightly lower. Australia and New Zealand (A/NZ) leverages its relative closeness to East Asia with strong trading relationships and treaties. Extraction industries and food exports match up well with rapidly growing, resource-starved East Asia. Also, the spike in commodity prices since 2010 has been favorable to all three countries, including Canada.

For technology acceptance, **Figure 48** illustrates the key indicators of wealth, population, total software market, and Internet usage:

Country	GDP per Person / Total GDP	# People (million)	Total Software Market		Internet Users		
			2010 Total / Tech Adopt.	2010-13 Forecasted Growth	Actual (million)	World Rank	% of People
U.S.	$46,900 $14,630 billion	312	$130.0 bill. advanced	5.4%	240	2	77%
Canada	$38,800 $ 1,330 billion	34	$ 9.8 billion advanced	5.8%	26	12	76%
Australia	$39,000 $ 880 billion	23	$ 4.0 billion advanced	7.0%	17	27	80%
New Zealand	$27,300 $ 120 billion	4	$ 0.4 billion advanced	6.8%	4	65	82%
3 Above	$38,000 $ 2,330 billion	61	$14.2 billion	6.2%	47		77%

Figure 48 – CANADA, AUSTRALIA, NEW ZEALAND: GDP, Population, Total Software Markets[x], Internet Usage[xi]

Canada, Australia, and New Zealand have high Internet usage. Additionally, the three countries combined have a total software market slightly less than the size of China or France's, which would be the sixth largest in the world if the three were a single country.

Examining the total software markets for these three countries graphically, **Figure 49** compares the total software market sizes by country to GDP PPP by country:

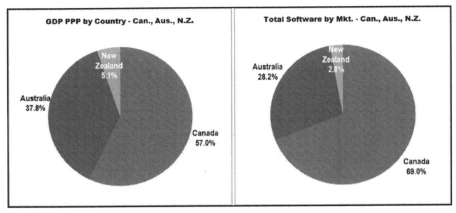

Figure 49 – CANADA, AUSTRALIA, NEW ZEALAND: GDP vs. Total Software Market Sizes

Figure 50 assesses the desirability of the Canada, Australia, and New Zealand's software markets, showing their software market shares compared to their GDP shares:

| Country | % of Total Can., Aus., N.Z. | | | Software Sales as % of GDP |
	Software Market Size	GDP PPP	Index (see footnote xxxviii)	
Canada	69.0%	57.4%	121	0.86%
Australia	28.2%	37.8%	75	0.65%
New Zealand	2.8%	5.1%	55	0.82%

Figure 50 – CANADA, AUSTRALIA, NEW ZEALAND: Comparison of GDP Share to Total Software Market Share

Of these three countries, Canada is the most software-intensive market.

Another approach to assessing technology acceptance across countries is the World Economic Forum's network readiness index (NRI), which was described directly before **Figure 7** on page 20 and a custom index to measure "readiness to embrace to enterprise software" on the same scale: 1 (low) to 7 (high). Illustrated below in **Figure 51** are the NRI and custom index results for Canada, Australia, New Zealand and other selected countries:

| | NRI Index | | | | | Custom Index: Enterprise Software (Scale of 1 to 7, low to high) | | | | | | | |
| | | | | | | 12.5% | 22.5% | 12.5% | 15.0% | 12.5% | 25.0% | 100% | |
	Index Score (1 - 7, LO-HI)	World Rank: '10-'11	Change: '10→'11	World Rank: '06-'07	Change: '07→'11	Avail. Of Latest Tech.	Laws Relating to ICT	Avail. - Scientists & Eng.	Buyer Sophistication	Extent of Staff Training	Co. Level of Tech. Absorp.	CUSTOM INDEX	CUSTOM INDEX, Canada = 100
"Rest of World"													
Canada	5.21	8	-1	11	3	6.4	5.5	5.6	4.7	5.0	5.6	5.47	100
Australia	5.06	17	-1	15	-2	6.1	5.5	4.5	4.4	4.8	5.9	5.30	97
New Zealand	5.03	18	1	22	4	6.0	5.5	4.1	4.0	4.8	5.9	5.18	95
Israel	4.81	22	6	18	-4	6.4	4.5	5.1	3.4	4.7	6.1	5.07	96
S. Africa	3.86	61	1	47	-14	5.5	4.8	3.3	4.1	4.7	5.4	4.73	89
Turkey	3.79	71	-2	52	-19	5.5	4.3	4.5	2.9	3.7	5.1	4.39	83
Selected Other Countries													
U.S.	5.33	5	0	7	2	6.4	5.4	5.7	4.5	5.1	6.0	5.54	101
Sweden	5.60	1	0	2	1	6.8	5.9	5.8	5.0	5.7	6.4	5.97	109
Norway	5.21	9	1	10	1	6.7	5.6	5.1	4.5	5.5	6.2	5.65	103
U.K.	5.12	15	-2	9	-6	6.4	5.4	4.8	4.6	4.7	5.7	5.32	97
France	4.92	20	-2	23	3	6.4	5.2	5.3	4.1	4.7	5.6	5.24	96
Brazil	3.90	56	5	53	-3	5.5	4.5	4.0	3.6	4.2	5.2	4.57	83
China	4.35	36	1	59	23	4.4	4.4	4.6	4.6	4.1	4.9	4.54	83
India	4.03	48	-5	44	-4	5.6	4.5	5.2	3.8	4.1	5.3	4.77	87
Indonesia	3.92	53	14	62	9	4.8	3.9	4.7	3.9	4.4	4.9	4.43	81
South Korea	5.19	10	5	19	9	6.1	5.1	4.9	4.6	4.4	6.1	5.29	97
India	4.03	48	-5	44	-4	5.6	4.5	5.2	3.8	4.1	5.3	4.77	87
China	4.35	36	1	59	23	4.4	4.4	4.6	4.6	4.1	4.9	4.54	83

Figure 51 – REST OF WORLD: NRI and Custom Enterprise Software Readiness Index

For both the standard NRI and the custom "readiness to embrace to enterprise software" index, Canada, Australia, and New Zealand rank high— in the top ten in the world for Canada and the top twenty for Australia and New Zealand. Their scores for both of these indices compare to those of U.S. and the large, advanced economies of Europe. This is not surprising, since they have the same wealth profile and attitudes toward technology as the U.S. and Europe.

Canada, Australia, and New Zealand: Technology Sales and Buying Culture

In the *Technology Sales and Buying Culture* dimension and availability of sales and technical staff, Canada, Australia, and New Zealand are similar and very close to the U.S. It is more expensive to employ staff in these countries, as taxes and social costs are as high as in Europe. Finally, technology buying behavior in Canada, Australia, and New Zealand in medium and enterprise organizations is more similar to the U.S. than any other countries in the world.

- **Canada**

  The supply of sales and technical talent is similar to the U.S. Note the comparable scores on the "availability of scientists and engineers" and "extent of staff training" indicators from **Figure 51** on page 117—all on a scale of 1 (low) to 7 (high)—5.6 and 5.0 for Canada and 5.7 and 5.1 for the U.S. Salaries in Canada are slightly higher, especially with the recent run up of the Canadian dollar versus the U.S. dollar. However, employment taxes and employer social security taxes are significantly higher in Canada than in the U.S.

  To measure buying behavior, the custom software indicators of "buyer sophistication" and "company level of technology absorption" from **Figure 51** on page 117 indicate Canadian scores of 4.7 and 5.6 versus U.S. scores of 4.5 and 6.0; again very similar.

- **Australia and New Zealand (A/NZ)**

  Australia and New Zealand's isolation has contributed to their strong technological base and infrastructure, as well as an adequate supply of sales and technical people. The seemingly geographical disadvantage of isolation has bred a favorable supply of potential sales and technical staff, rivaling the U.S. Furthermore, Australia is building a nationwide fiber-optic high-speed Internet network, called the National Broadband Network.[xxxix] This will provide Internet connection speeds up to one gigabit per second to 93% of the businesses and households in Australia. A/NZ has a very similar culture and tech buying behavior to the U.S. and Canada.

  Similar to Canada, buying behavior is measured by using the custom software indicators of "buyer sophistication" and "company level of technology absorption" from **Figure 51** on page 117. This shows the following score comparisons to the U.S.:

- Buyer Sophistication (on the same 1–7 scale, low to high): Australia and New Zealand are 4.4 and 4.0 respectively, compared to the U.S. at 4.5.
- Company Level of Technology Absorption: Australia and New Zealand are 5.9 each, just below the U.S. at 6.0. One of the major factors of A/NZ companies being so willing to invest in technology to improve their business processes is their geographic isolation.

To quantify the top segments for technology spending in Canada, Australia and New Zealand, **Figure 52** illustrates the breakdown of total technology spending by vertical segment for the three countries with the U.S. added for comparison:

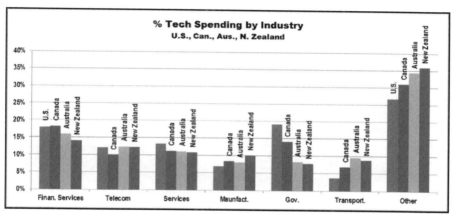

Figure 52 – Total Technology Spending[xxii] by Leading Industry Segments: U.S., Canada, Australia, New Zealand

Surprisingly, the only segment for total technology spending with significant variance between the countries is in government spending. The U.S. and Canadian government spend 19% and 14%, respectively, of total tech spending, while Australia and New Zealand spend approximately 9% each. Additionally, the U.S. is much lower in spending in the transportation segment that the others.

See the "**Implications – Approach to Market Entry**" sections below, at the bottom of page 120 for Canada and page 122 for Australia and New Zealand.

Putting It All Together – Canada, Australia, New Zealand

Across the 4 Dimensions of Country Analysis, **Figure 53** illustrates the similarity of Canada, Australia, and New to the U.S.; the most alike of all the countries in the world.

Country / Region	Category & US$ GDP Per Person	# People	Total Software Market			English for Language of Commerce?	Tech Sales & Buying Culture
			2010 ($ billion) – Tech. Adoption	2010-13 Forecasted Growth			
Canada	Wealthy $38,800	34.3 million	$9.8 advanced	5.8%		Yes, except for Quebec with French	• Very close to U.S. in buying culture and similar business culture • Strong supply of sales & tech talent • Comparable compensation & higher employment costs than U.S.
Australia + New Zealand	Wealthy $37,100	27.0 million	$4.4 advanced	7.0%		Yes – native	• Other than Canada, most similar to N. America in buying and business culture • Strong supply of sales & tech talent; developed, self-sufficient tech culture because of geographic isolation • Comparable compensation & higher employment costs than U.S.
U.S.	Top $46,900	312.1 million	$130.0 advanced	5.4%			

Figure 53 – CANADA, AUSTRALIA, NEW ZEALAND: Summary of 4 Dimensions for Country Evaluation

Implications – Approach to Market Entry for Canada

When considering international expansion, most enterprise software vendors consider Canada a special case since is it contiguous to the U.S. and very similar in both business environment and in all 4 Dimensions for Country Evaluation. The only significant difference from the U.S. in selling enterprise software into Canada is the French language, primarily spoken in the province of Quebec, where 80% of the population is French-speaking. Quebec makes up approximately 23% of Canada's population and 20% of Canada's GDP. Some consider Quebec residents radical in their desire to preserve their French-speaking culture, and in the last twenty-five years this province has held two referendums on succession from Canada. The estimates are that 30% to 40% of Quebec residents still support succession.

For direct sales, enterprise software vendors usually consider Canada as an extension of the U.S. The vast majority of Canadians live within 100 miles of the U.S. border, and many of the targets for enterprise software—medium and enterprise organizations—are located in the top twelve major metro areas, listed in **Figure 54:**

Metro Area + Nearby Areas in the Top 12	Population[xi] (millions)	Population (% of Total Canada)	Nearest Major U.S. Business Center
Toronto + Surrounding Areas	7.3	21%	Detroit Boston, New York, Chicago roughly equidistant, twice as far as Detroit
Montreal + Surrounding Areas	5.5	16%	Boston, New York
Calgary, Edmonton	2.1	6%	Seattle, but not really that close, since these cities are directly north of Montana
Winnipeg	0.7	2%	Minneapolis
Vancouver, Victoria	2.5	7%	Seattle
TOTAL – Top 12 Metro Areas	18.1	53%	

Figure 54 – Top 12 Canadian Metro Areas by Population

Since all the Canadian metro areas listed above, with the exception of Calgary/Edmonton, are within 75 miles of the U.S. border, Canadian software sales offices can serve as branches to the nearest sales office in the U.S. business centers listed above. Alternatively, a Toronto-based sales office can cover Toronto, Montreal, and their surrounding areas, which together comprise 37% of Canada's population. These two metro areas contain more than half of the enterprise businesses in Canada, with the exception of the energy industry, which has a large presence in both Calgary and Edmonton.

The French language issue in Quebec is significant. 80% of Quebec residents claim French as their native language compared to only 8% for English. In the Montreal metro area, which has a higher English-speaking percentage than in the province overall, two-thirds speak only French[xli]. It is clear that selling into Quebec, accounting for approximately 20% of total Canadian GDP, requires French-speaking sales/technology staff or channel partners, as well as software translated into French.

Aside from the French language differences, non-direct sales channels such as telesales, Internet, and channel partners are virtually the same as in the U.S. It certainly doesn't hurt to have Canadian channel partners, but Canadian enterprise organizations are accustomed to buying from the U.S. Other than Canadian laws requiring both French and English on packaged software and the need for French help files for Quebec clients, there are no barriers to importing U.S. software into Canada.

Implications – Approach to Market Entry for Australia and New Zealand

As was described in the previous sections, Australia and New Zealand are similar to Canada, as they have the same wealth profile, technology acceptance, and technology sales/buying culture as the U.S. Combined they are approximately 75% the size of Canada in terms of GDP and population, but less than the half the size of Canada in their total software markets. However, their geographic remoteness and awkward time zones make them difficult to start up and manage from the U.S. For this reason, a reasonable approach for enterprise software vendors is to begin selling in A/NZ when starting up in Southeast Asia. Singapore is five hours by plane from Perth, the largest city on the west coast of Australia, and eight hours from Sydney or Melbourne, which is relatively close for this part of the world. Regarding time zones, depending on the season, Sydney is two to three hours ahead of Singapore.

7 THE REST OF THE WORLD

Introduction

The preceding chapters of this book described and analyzed the major regions of the world for enterprise software vendors to consider expansion: Europe, East Asia, Latin America, and finally Canada, Australia, New Zealand as a single unit. This final chapter considers the most developed countries from the Rest of the World: Russia, Eastern Europe, Central Asia, the Middle East, Africa, and the Caribbean.

The countries in the Rest of the World combined represent a GDP PPP of approximately 15% of the world's total and almost 2 billion people or 28% of the world's population. In this group, there is vast, lawless Russia and a few small, noncontiguous territories with potential to be profitable enterprise software markets at some point: Israel, South Africa, and Turkey. The rest are considered developing countries, not mature or advanced enough to support enterprise software sales. No negative connotation is intended, just that these developing countries are the last for enterprise software vendors to consider for sales expansion.

Figure 55 lists 2010 GDP PPP and population for notable countries from these parts of the world:

	GDP using PPP (US $ billions)				Population (millions)				GDP (PPP) / Person (calculated)		
	World Rank	US$ (billion)	% of This Section	% of World	World Rank	People (millions)	% of This Section	% of World	US $	Rank On List	Index (World Avg. = 100)
"Other"											
Russia	6	2,223	20.2%	3.00%	9	142.9	7.3%	2.1%	15,556	4	145
Turkey	16	961	8.7%	1.30%	18	73.7	3.8%	1.1%	13,039	5	122
Saudi Arabia	23	620	5.6%	0.84%	46	27.1	1.4%	0.4%	22,878	3	213
S. Africa	25	524	4.8%	0.71%	25	50.0	2.6%	0.7%	10,480	6	98
Israel	49	218	2.0%	0.29%	95	7.7	0.4%	0.1%	28,312	2	264
United Arab Emirates (UAE)	53	187	1.7%	0.25%	117	4.7	0.2%	0.1%	39,787	1	371
TOTAL - Rest of World		6,261	56.9%	8.46%		1,646.0	84.3%	23.9%	3,804		35
TOTAL - 7 Above		$ 10,994	100.0%	14.9%		1,952	100.0%	28.3%	$ 5,632		53

Figure 55 – REST OF THE WORLD: Top Markets Ranked by 2010 GDP PPP

The six countries listed above combined have a software market slightly less than that of Canada, but are forecasted to grow at more than twice the annual rate of the U.S. and Canada for 2010-2013.

Figure 56 illustrates 2010 total software markets and 2010-2013 forecasted growth rates for these six countries with Canada and the U.S. added for reference. It also shows percentages of regional and world totals:

Country	2010 Total Software Market ($ billions)	Total Software as % of GDP	Software Market % of Total		2010 – 2013 Forecasted Growth	2013 Forecast	
			% These 6 Countries	% World		Total Software Market ($ billions)	% World
U.S.	$129.95	0.88%	> 11x	40.0%	5.4%	$152.0	37.2%
Canada	$ 9.81	0.68%	106.2%	3.0%	5.8%	$11.6	2.8%
Russia	$ 3.69	0.26%	33.4%	1.13%	12.0%	$ 5.18	1.26%
Turkey	$ 1.01	0.16%	9.1%	0.31%	12.0%	$ 1.41	0.34%
Saudi Arabia	$ 0.96	0.23%	8.6%	0.29%	12.5%	$ 1.36	0.33%
South Africa	$ 2.50	0.69%	22.5%	0.77%	11.1%	$ 3.42	0.83%
Israel	$ 0.80	0.42%	7.2%	0.25%	13.2%	$ 1.16	0.28%
UAE	$ 0.30	0.14%	2.7%	0.09%	19.8%	$ 0.52	0.13%

Country	2010 Total Software Market ($ billions)	Total Software as % of GDP	Software Market % of Total		2010 – 2013 Forecasted Growth	2013 Forecast	
			% These 6 Countries	% World		Total Software Market ($ billions)	% World
6 Above	$ 9.24		83.6%	2.84%	12.2%	$13.05	3.18%
Rest of World	$ 1.82		16.4%	0.56%	12.0%	$ 2.55	0.62%
6 + Rest of World	$11.06		100.0%	3.40%	12.1%	$15.60	3.80%

Figure 56 – OTHER COUNTRIES: 2010-2013 Total Software Market, Growth Rates, % of Total Region & World

South Africa and Israel's total software markets stand out for being larger than their GDP's would suggest:

- **South Africa** – its GDP PPP is only 4.8% of the total for the six countries plus the Rest of the World, yet its total software market is proportionally much larger at 22.5% of the total combined software markets in this group of countries. This results in a huge index of software market share to GDP of 473.

- **Israel** – its GDP PPP is 2.0% of the total of the countries in the table above, yet its total combined software market is also proportionally much larger at 7.2% of the total, resulting in an index of 364;

- **The Rest of the World** – all the rest of the countries combined, excluding the top six in this group, only have an index of 29; that is, their total software market share is 29% of their total GDP PPP share.

Since these six countries are usually not considered by enterprise software vendors until Europe, East Asia and Latin America are already operating, rather than consider the 4 Dimensions for Country Evaluation, each country will be summarized to discuss its current challenges and why it is not ready for market entry consideration. They are ranked from highest to lowest potential.

1. **Russia**

Despite being the largest country by far in this group and one of the BRICS countries (see footnote [v] on page 135), Russia today is a very difficult place for operating a business due to the lack of an organized business infrastructure and inconsistent enforcement of laws, which have only existed since the late 1990s. However, it is supposedly much better than it was immediately after the collapse of the Soviet Union in 1991. For a software vendor this is a particularly difficult environment, as IP protection for software is impossible to enforce and the percentage of pirated software hovers around 70%, ranked 62nd in the world for this NRI indicator[xlii]. This compares with a 79% piracy rate for China and a 65% rate for India.

The probability of legal or democratic reforms is low, as Vladimir Putin has been in power for eleven years, despite placing a weak protégé as President in 2008. Putin is widely criticized for his anti-democratic, strong-armed tactics and the official crime and "thuggery" against political opponents that still exists in Russia. Notwithstanding this grim assessment, Russia is a worldwide leader in natural resource production and exports. It is also a leading military and diplomatic power and it has the largest stockpile of nuclear weapons in the world. On the negative side, the lifespan of Russian citizens has decreased to the level of the least developed countries in the world, which contributed to a population decline from 149 million in 1991 to 143 million today. The population decline has stabilized with increasing birth rates and fewer people emigrating from Russia to find better economic prospects.

2. **Israel**

Despite its small population of 7.7 million, Israel is a technology leader. Its GDP per person is climbing toward the *Wealthy* range and is currently at US $28,300 per person. Its startling success in technology start-ups has resulted in Israel having the second most NASDAQ listed companies after the U.S. and is chronicled in the book: *Start-up Nation: The Story of Israel's Economic Miracle*[xliii].

The primary barriers to enterprise software vendors selling into Israel are its small size and unbeatable competition from local Israeli firms in many facets of software, including enterprise. For those few segments where Israeli companies don't produce software, enterprise software vendors sell through Israeli channel and sales partners. This is the only way to sell in Israel because of the tight connections between Israelis in its business community formed during their mandatory military service after high school. These connections are one of the major success factors cited in the book above for the success of Israeli technology start-ups.

3. South Africa

With a GDP per person of US $10,500, South Africa is not currently wealthy enough for market entry consideration, but it has potential. Though its government has been a democracy with black majority rule for twenty years, it is still a bifurcated economy with white's median income approximately six times the median black income, and unemployment rates of white males at 4% versus 25% for black males. Despite this lingering racial division, South Africa is the most highly developed economy in Africa and has large reserves of high-value minerals, such as diamonds, gold, and platinum. It has a large target market of sophisticated enterprise companies in financial services, manufacturing, and mining, to name a few industries. English is the language of commerce in these large enterprises.

South Africa's location at the southern tip of Africa is a disadvantage, as it is far away from any other major markets for enterprise software.

4. Turkey

This is a secular Muslim state that was formed from the remnants of the Ottoman Empire after its defeat in World War I. Its wealth and technology acceptance are both too low to be considered for market entry by enterprise software vendors: its GDP per person of US $13,000 places it in the lower part of *Middle Income*, and its NRI index score is 3.79 on the scale of 1 (low) to 7 (high), ranked 71st in the world.

Turkey straddles categories on several dimensions, both geographically and politically, as well as just emerging from *Developing* to *Middle Income* on the GDP per person scale in **Figure 4** on page 14.

- Located on the southeast corner of Europe, a sliver of its territory is in Europe (around its major business center, Istanbul), but the majority of its territory is in extreme southwest Asia.

- It is a Muslim country, but the most secular and democratic of the Muslim states in the Middle East.

- Turkey has close military and political relations with Israel, which confirms it as a political outsider.

- It is a stalwart member of the political/military alliance of NATO, but still has rocky relations with its traditional enemy Greece, a fellow NATO member. A sign of the cold relations with Greece is the stalemate on the Island of Cyprus, an EU member, which has been divided into Greek and Turkish factions with separate governments since 1974.

Turkey has been trying to join the European Union (EU) for 25 years, with opposition coming from many fronts:

- Those that don't want Turkey to have so many EU voting seats because of its large population of 74 million. Turkey's population is 90% of Germany's, which is the most populous EU member
- Concerns among members having a majority Muslim state in the EU
- Opposition from its historic enemies, already EU members: Greece and Austria
- Turkey's occupation of Cyprus, also an EU member.

Turkey truly is a crossroads country, which makes it geographically and militarily more important than its small economic footprint might indicate.

5. Saudi Arabia, United Arab Emirates, and Rest of the Arab Middle East

Saudi Arabia has the largest GDP PPP in the Middle East at US $620 billion, one-quarter the size of one of the large European economies, with GDP per person at US $22,800 in the *Upper Middle Income* category of GDP per person. This is due to its enormous oil wealth and little else. Several tiny Arab countries—most notably the United Arab Emirates (UAE) and Qatar—have very high GDPs per person fed by huge oil wealth: UAE (4.7 million people) at almost US $40,000; and tiny Qatar (1.7 million people) the highest in the world at almost US $90,000. Most of the Arab countries are hindered by having absolute monarchies as dictators, some relatively benevolent and others outright tyrannical. Many of these rulers are teetering, with the overthrow of governments in Algeria and the most populous Arab country, Egypt.

Selling enterprise software in these Arab monarchies requires pay-offs to a member of the ruling family, which is in direct contradiction to the U.S. Foreign Corrupt Practices Act. To get around these roadblocks, U.S. laws require forgoing direct sales in favor of channels or sales partners who have connections to the ruling family. There are very few enterprise software prospects in these countries outside the oil industry and the large banks.

8 SUMMARY – ENTIRE WORLD

The wealthiest countries with the highest tech acceptance are the U.S., the large European countries, Canada, and Australia/New Zealand. After Canada, U.S. enterprise software vendors tend to start international expansion into Europe because of its wealth, tech acceptance, and geographic concentration. Northern Europe, which includes the UK and the artificial regional constructs of Benelux and Scandinavia plus Finland, are usually the first markets enterprise software vendors consider as they tend to have the highest technology acceptance and more English-speaking decision-makers for purchasing enterprise software. After Northern Europe, translating software enables expansion into Germany, France, Spain, and Italy.

After Europe, many enterprise software vendors consider East Asia because of its rapid economic growth and development, huge populations, and exceptional potential. However, each East Asian market/region is challenging for enterprise software vendors on multiple levels. Each of the four major regions of East Asia[xliv] has a unique culture, customs and business practices and—other than India and Singapore—few English-speaking individuals. Enterprise software vendors that have had the most success in East Asia hire or retain people with experience selling and marketing enterprise software there. Australia and New Zealand (A/NZ) are sometimes added on to East Asia because of their close trading relationships and time zones, forming an Asia Pacific region. A/NZ, which can be considered as a unit, is next door to East Asia, but its wealth and technology acceptance is more similar to the U.S., Canada, and the large European countries. The biggest challenge is justifying start-up in A/NZ because their GDPs and populations are quite small. Combined, Australia and New Zealand together are only three-quarters the size of Canada.

Latin America has historically been approached after Europe and East Asia because of its low wealth, geographic isolation, poor business environments as a result of government bias against businesses, and Spanish/Portuguese language requirements. However, after a decade of steady movement to democracy, strong economic growth, and the emergence of Brazil as the seventh largest economy in the world, Latin America is becoming increasingly attractive. Nevertheless, its total and per capita GDP is only one-third that of Europe or the U.S. Also, its second and third largest economies, Mexico and Argentina, are experiencing significant difficulties, which make them unsuitable for enterprise software expansion: Mexico is mired in a war with drug cartels that puts non-Mexicans at risk and Argentina is suffering from persistent economic weakness and is saddled with poor economic planning.

Canada, which is the most similar to the U.S. across the 4 Dimensions of Country Evaluation, can be approached independently of any other international territory as an extension to the U.S. sales offices. Australia and New Zealand, also very similar to the U.S., are usually started when enterprise software sales commence in Southeast Asia.

9 ABOUT THE AUTHOR

Jay Greenwald is the Managing Partner for International Revenue *ACCELERATION*, a consultancy that helps on-premise enterprise, SaaS, and Cloud software vendors expand their sales, channels, and go-to-market capabilities outside their home countries. This consultancy has relationships with experienced software salespeople and general managers all over the world, ready to help software vendors implement their expansion programs. Mr. Greenwald's personal enterprise software sales, channel, product, and merger and acquisition (M&A) experience spans 65 countries.

Mr. Greenwald was born in France to American parents. He has lived in London, Paris, and Singapore and has traveled to 41 countries to sell and motivate others to sell software. When he is not traveling outside the U.S., he lives in beautiful Denver, Colorado, U.S. with his wife, who is also an entrepreneur, his three teenage daughters, and two dogs.

Mr. Greenwald earned his MBA from Harvard Business School. He has worked in every function within a software company, including worldwide general management, sales/channel management and consulting roles.

NOTES

[i] Purchasing power parity (PPP) is used for GDP throughout this book, which is the best way to compare markets for enterprise software. GDP PPP adjusts a country's GDP number for the price levels in that country. This contrasts with nominal GDP, which translate a country's GDP into a common currency, usually U.S. dollars at the current exchange rate.

[ii] *Digital Planet 2010*, World Technology and Services Alliances

[iii] Source is speedtest.net, which has 2.1 billion Internet speed tests in its database, and a map displaying worldwide Internet usage by showing lights.

[iv] Technically Mexico, Central America, and the Caribbean countries are part of North America. In terms of the regions outlined in this book, Mexico and Central America will be classified as part of Latin America, and the Caribbean countries will be part of the developing countries in the Rest of the World.

[v] BRICS Countries are Brazil, Russia, India, China and South Africa, which was recently added, though it is a good deal smaller than the others. These are rapidly growing countries at a similar stage of development, quickly moving from the developing to developed world.

[vi] 2010 GDP PPP as listed by the International Monetary Fund (IMF) from Wikipedia

[vii] International Monetary Fund

[viii] Source is IMF's 2010 GDP PPP. Note that none of the top category countries has a large population other than the U.S., which has the largest GDP per person of the large countries.

[ix] A semi-autonomous region of China since 1999, not a separate country.

[x] *Digital Planet 2010*, World Technology and Services Alliances

[xi] Internet usage data is from the Internet Word Stats, http://www.Internetworldstats.com/. This web site says there were 1.8 billion Internet users in the world as of 12/31/2009, 27% of the world's total population.

[xii] The World Economic Forum and Insead, a top international business school, produce an annual report entitled *The Global Information Technology Report* (*http://reports.weforum.org/global-information-technology-report/ and the 435-*

page (!) PDF version: http://reports.weforum.org/global-information-technology-report/content/pdf/wef-gitr-2010-2011.pdf).

[xiii] World Economic Forum, *The Global Information Technology Report*, page ix, first paragraph.

[xiv] "Environment" sub-index is made up of market environment, political and regulatory framework, and infrastructure environment qualitative and quantitative measures

[xv] "Readiness" sub-index is made up of individual citizen readiness, business readiness and government readiness qualitative and quantitative measures

[xvi] "Usage" sub-index is made up of individual citizen usage, business usage and government usage qualitative and quantitative measures

[xvii] Note that the GDP numbers per person for the rest of this book don't tie exactly to the numbers listed in **Figure 4**, on page 14. The minor differences are due to methodology calculating GDP PPP per person.

[xviii] Note that the total line includes 20 more small countries for a total GDP PPP of US $844 billion and population of 72 million people.

[xix] Index value of greater than 100 means country's share of European total software market is greater than that country's share of total European GDP

[xx] Wikipedia, *"Financial Centre"*

[xxi] Wikipedia, *"World City"*

[xxii] Technology spending is the total of hardware, software, computer services and communications spending from *Digital Planet 2010*, from the World Technology and Services Alliance. It is sometimes referred to as Information and Communications Technology (ICT) spending.

[xxiii] Note that the total line includes 10 additional small countries totaling GDP PPP of US $567 billion and a population of 280 million people.

[xxiv] This is nominal GDP, not GDP PPP as is used in this book. In PPP terms, China GDP is 2.5 times that of Japan.

[xxv] Wikipedia, *"Hong Kong"*

[xxvi] *Wall Street Journal*, 17 March 2011, "China Mobile Slugs Out a Profit." Contrast this with Japan, where 75% of cell phone users access the Internet from their cell phones.

[xxvii] *Forbes Money Builder*, 24 June 2010, from a 2009 study (http://blogs.forbes.com/moneybuilder/2010/06/24/one-big-difference-between-chinese-and-american-households-debt/).

[xxviii] 12 March 2011, "Bamboo Capitalism," page 13, paragraphs 4 and 6.

[xxix] Index value of greater than 100 means country's share of East Asian total software market is greater than that country's share of East Asian total GDP

[xxx] From a 1996 Census, *ICE Hong Kong*, University College London.

[xxxi] Wikipedia, *"Financial Centre"*

[xxxii] Wikipedia, *"Largest Ports"*

[xxxiii] Indian Government, 2005 Economic Census.

[xxxiv] Note that the total line includes 12 more small countries for a total GDP PPP of US $473 billion and total population of 67 million people.

[xxxv] Report from The Inter-American Development Bank in 1999

[xxxvi] Wikipedia, *"BRIC"*

[xxxvii] Index value of greater than 100 means country's share of the Latin American total software market is greater than that country's share of total Latin American GDP

[xxxviii] Index value of greater than 100 means country's share of the Canada, Australia, New Zealand total software market is greater than that country's share of total GDP of these three countries

[xxxix] Wikipedia *"National Broadband Network"*

[xl] Census Metropolitan Area (CMA) in Canada, which has its last national census in 2006

[xli] http://montreal.citystar.com/mall/montreal_facts.html

[xlii] The World Economic Forum, *The Global Information Technology Report 2010-2011* page 268, item 2.08.

[xliii] *Start-Up Nation*, by Dan Senor and Saul Singer

[xliv] (1) China (2) India (3) NE Asia: Japan and S. Korea (4) SE Asia: Singapore, Malaysia, Indonesia, Philippines

Made in the USA
San Bernardino, CA
19 March 2016